GOD, NEIGHBOR, EMPIRE

GOD, NEIGHBOR, EMPIRE

*The Excess of Divine Fidelity and the Command
of Common Good*

Walter Brueggemann

BAYLOR UNIVERSITY PRESS

Cover Design by Hannah Feldmeier

Library of Congress Cataloging-in-Publication Data

Names: Brueggemann, Walter, author.
Title: God, neighbor, empire : the excess of divine fidelity and
the command of common good / Walter Brueggemann.
Description: Waco : Baylor University Press, 2016.
Identifiers: LCCN 2016006232 (print) | LCCN 2016031875
(ebook) | ISBN 9781481305426 (hardback) | ISBN 9781481306034
(web pdf) | ISBN 9781481306027 (mobi) |
ISBN 9781481305440 (epub)
Subjects: LCSH: Christianity—Essence, genius, nature. |
Justice—Biblical teaching. | Law—Biblical teaching. | Grace
(Theology)—Biblical teaching.
Classification: LCC BT60 .B78 2016 (print) | LCC BT60 (ebook)
| DDC 230—dc23
LC record available at https://lccn.loc.gov/2016006232

for Scott Matheney

with gratitude and affection

CONTENTS

FOREWORD

As we navigate the clamor of our culture wars, the church needs wise guides. They need to be biblically rooted, prophetically clear, and pastorally compassionate. For decades, Walter Brueggemann has been one such guide.

Throughout his life, he has called the church to exercise prophetic imagination. In these essays he calls us to *prophetic listening*. He demonstrates that Scripture expresses the continual dialogue between God and people, as God listens to the cries of the poor, and the prophetic leaders of Israel listen to the heart of God.

Our lives are inundated by the noise of discordant opinions. This noise lures us to pursue our own special interests, and to wall us off from neighbors, especially those who seem strange or threatening. Brueggemann demonstrates over and again the call to renew our careful listening to God and our neighbor. This will make us more credible and fruitful as witnesses to the God of faithful love—and more equipped to live with faithful obedience in the world.

In his unique gifts as an exegete, prophet, and pastor, he woos us to the heart of God, and through that seeks to open our hearts more fully to our neighbors, our strangers, and even our enemies.

Though government legislatures are charged to write just laws that further the common good, they are often dominated by special interests, divided over ideology, and at times brought to a standstill over disagreements about the primacy of individual freedom versus government legislation. Furthermore, partisan positions over issues of justice are central to political campaigns and their funding. Add to this the tragic reality that denominations and congregations are now divided over not only ethnicity and worship ethos but ethics—and it is easy to see why we lack clear moral leadership that draws us together as a society.

At Fuller Theological Seminary, we discerned that church leaders need opportunities to reflect on the integration of justice, grace, and law in the mission of God. We believe that God wants our individual and corporate lives to be shaped more by careful reading of Scripture and faithful listening to the Spirit than they are by our social context or media-shaped ideology. We focused a conference for church leaders around this theme, and there was no one better suited to provide biblical reflections than Walter Brueggemann. We gave him a complex task—to lead us in understanding the relationship of justice, grace, and law for followers of Christ as we participate in God's mission in the world. His addresses challenged, inspired, and stunned. We are grateful that his rich insights, in expanded form, are now available to a wider public.

Brueggemann wrestles the contested terms of justice, grace, and law away from the world of the courtroom into the house of love. He demonstrates how, biblically, they are relational words, descriptors of lives lived in loving fidelity to the God of faithful love. Even law serves the purpose of guarding relationships, and our obedience is a response to God's faithful love toward us. Brueggemann orients our pursuit of justice to a passion for the common good, not just for the right application of law.

He liberates justice from the all-too-common Aristotelian notion of retribution—or something viewed in contrast to grace—to a much richer meaning as the "socioeconomic, political order that makes neighborly solidarity possible and available to all." Through detailed engagement with Scripture, Brueggemann demonstrates that just as the psalmist declared that love, faithfulness, righteousness, and peace will kiss (Ps 85:10-13), so justice, grace, and law embrace each other in our relationships of fidelity to God and one another.

With penetrating insight, he parallels the self-serving domestication of justice by the ruling elite in Israel with the misuse of justice by those in power today who misuse it to safeguard their control and luxury at the expense of the common people. He demonstrates that the God of justice relentlessly pursues the well-being of those "below," expressed in the continual command for Israel to guard the widow, orphan, and stranger. Remember, we once were also strangers and slaves.

In his development of the Decalogue, Brueggemann demonstrates that the law is an expression of God's grace, rescuing Israel from slavery. The law is God's gift to keep Israel out of bondage, expressing God's call to Israel to recast all relationships in justice for the good of all.

At the heart of this recasting is the affirmation that we are called to fidelity. Fidelity requires face-to-face relationships in which promises are kept and the common good is pursued. Brueggemann calls this *othering*—looking after the good of the other. In our society, we are so easily seduced into fixating on our selves, on *selfing*. The call to fidelity turns our lives inside out. These face-to-face neighborly relationships pull us out of isolation and enmity. God's faithful love transforms all our social relationships, extending to neighbor, stranger, and even enemy. This isn't mere rhetoric or a lofty ideal. Rather, neighborliness has tangible expression in lending generously, conducting all affairs justly, and distributing freely to those in need, even—and possibly especially—to strangers, outcasts, and enemies.

Rather than simply encouraging us to be more combatants who bruise others in our culture wars, this book guides us to new forms of culture care as we are empowered by the Spirit to participate in God's great love for our neighbors.

Dr. Tim A. Dearborn, Director
Lloyd John Ogilvie Institute of Preaching
Fuller Theological Seminary

PREFACE

These several chapters were presented as lectures at Fuller Seminary. I was very glad for the invitation to Fuller, as it gave me a chance and an impetus to think through the themes I have exposited here. As is usual with my work, I have intended that there should be an edge of contemporaneity to my exposition, and no doubt the Fuller invitation intended that. My judgment is that the themes of relationality exposited here are of immense urgency in a society that has largely reduced social relationships to commodity and technique. There is no doubt that the witness of Scripture is a mighty protest against such reduction that was as acute in the ancient world as in our own time. Scripture, moreover, in insistent and imaginative ways, goes beyond critical protest to commend alternative practices that are "impractical" but non-negotiably urgent for a viable, flourishing society.

I so much enjoyed my time at Fuller Seminary where I was generously hosted by Tim Dearborn and seriously engaged by President Mark Labberton. I benefitted from the thoughtful competence of Victoria Smith and enjoyed attentive interaction with my generous minder, Reed Metcalf. On all counts, including worship in the seminary community and responses from faculty colleagues, it was a happy time for me and a welcome stimulus for my own thinking.

My debts to many colleagues are evident in the notes. I thank in particular Davis Hankins, who read through and critiqued the manuscript in helpful ways, and James Boyd White, whose work has led me into new thinking about the dialogic character of law. As usual, I am indebted to the press and its staff—especially Jordan Rowan Fannin, Cade Jarrell, and Diane Smith—who take such good care of words that can be transposed into a book.

I am glad to dedicate this study to Scott Matheney, long-time chaplain at my alma mater, Elmhurst College. Scott is an engine for passion and energy in faith. He has guided, mentored, and summoned generations of students at Elmhurst College to critical, active, responsible gospel faith with verve, courage, and imagination.

Walter Brueggemann
World Wide Communion Sunday, 2015

INTRODUCTION

Biblical texts always emerged in a context. We often cannot determine with any precision the exact historical moment or circumstance of such emergence of any particular text. But we can determine, very often, the macro-context of political economy for such emergence, for the patterns of political economy in the ancient world are recurring. Specifically, much of the Old Testament text emerged in contexts of empire amid great concentrations of wealth and power. Thus, we are able to trace a sequence of empires and their impact in the Old Testament from the paradigmatic empire of Pharaoh in Egypt to the Assyrian, Babylonian, and Persian empires, to the global power of Alexander the Great and his Hellenistic successors, and finally to the Roman Empire. This sequence, in large sweep, was interrupted in ancient Israel only by the modest empire of Solomon (the Davidic dynasty) that presided over the Jerusalem establishment for a long period of time.[1]

Given some particularities, it is fair to say that ancient empires, like contemporary empires, can be identified by recurring markers. For our purposes we may identify three

1

characteristic marks of imperial policy and practice. First, empires existed to extract wealth in order to transfer wealth from the vulnerable to the powerful. (Solomon's practice of extraction featured an imposing taxation system. See 1 Kings 4:7-19 and the revolt against his taxation system in 1 Kings 12:1-19.) Second, empires pursued a policy of commoditization in which everything and everyone was reduced to a dispensable commodity that could be bought and sold and traded and possessed and consumed. (Solomon's practice of commoditization is evident in his policy of forced labor [1 Kgs 5:13; 9:20-22] and his expansive trade policies that produced seemingly limitless wealth for his entourage [1 Kgs 10:13-25].) Third, empires that practiced extraction and commoditization were fully prepared to undertake violence on whatever scale was required for the success of extraction and commoditization. (For Solomon, the combination of taxation, slavery, and confiscatory trade constituted a state policy in readiness for violence.) All such policies and practices could be justified as they secured the expansive wealth of the empire.

These policies and practices, moreover, were regularly legitimated by liturgical enactment of myths that allied the power of God to the power of the state. Such an understanding of god (gods) was perforce top-down, so that the claims of empire were theologically imposed by the empire of force.[2] The gods whom the liturgy attested were champions of extraction and commoditization in the service of a coherent social order. That social order eventually came to be accepted as normal and normative by the populace, so that extraction and commoditization came to be viewed as routine:

> In a situation of assured power, with unchallengeable hegemony, an empire does not need to use military force.[3]

Such hegemony, performed as normative liturgy, becomes the "common sense limit" of ordinary life beyond which it is not possible to imagine. The god (gods) celebrated in the imperial liturgy assured the legitimacy, normalcy, and ordinariness of such policy and practice.

It is in that recurring, almost constant context of empire that the Old Testament became the countertext of ancient Israel. The Old Testament is offered as an alternative to the imperial narrative that dominates ordinary imagination. That countertext intends to subvert the dominant imperial text and so is rightly seen as a "sub-version." The trajectory of texts that the synagogue and the church entertain as "good news" bears witness to an emancipatory God who stands apart from and over against the mythic claims of imperial religion.[4] The God attested in the Exodus narrative, the covenantal tradition of Deuteronomy, and the prophetic corpus stands over against the ideology of empire. The paradigmatic narrative of Exodus–sojourn–Sinai, presided over by Moses, yields an alternative narrative that is occupied by an alternative God:

- The Exodus narrative (Exod 1–15) exhibits Yhwh—in the service of emancipation and the end of economic extraction—as more powerful than the Egyptian gods (see Exod 12:12).
- The narrative of wilderness sojourn (Exod 16–18)—with the surprising gifts of abundant water, bread, and meat—witnesses against the usurpatious ideology of scarcity that propels Pharaoh. The wilderness narrative teems with abundance for all for all.
- The meeting at Sinai yields a covenantal relationship wherein Yhwh and the people of Yhwh pledge abiding fidelity to each other (Exod 19–24):

> This very day the Lord your God is commanding you to observe these statutes and ordinances; so observe them diligently with all your heart and with all your soul. Today you have obtained the Lord's agreement: to be your God, and for you to walk in his ways, to keep his statutes, his commandments, and his ordinances, and to obey him. Today the Lord has obtained your agreement: to be his treasured people,

3

as he promised you, and to keep his commandments;
for him to set you high above all nations that he has
made, in praise and in fame, and in honor; and for
you to be a people holy to the Lord your God, as he
promised. (Deut 26:16-19)

In sum we are able to see that the *emancipatory narrative* of
Exodus, the *abundance* attested in the wilderness, and the *covenant of Sinai* provide a very different account of lived reality in
the world due to the decisive agency of Yhwh. In each of these
episodes in the narrative, it is the newly engaged God, Yhwh,
who makes the decisive difference. Yhwh is unlike the gods of
the empire; Yhwh has no interest in extraction:

Not for your sacrifices do I rebuke you;
your burnt offerings are continually before me.
I will not accept a bull from your house, or goats from
    your folds.
For every wild animal of the forest is mine,
the cattle on a thousand hills.
I know all the birds of the air,
and all that moves in the field is mine. (Ps 50:8-11)

Yhwh values human community and human persons, and
refuses the reduction of even the vulnerable to the status of
dispensable commodity:

You shall not deprive a resident alien or an orphan of justice;
you shall not take a widow's garment in pledge. (Deut 24:17)

This God, as given in the narrative, is not immune to the practice of violence, but the narrative of this God is on a trajectory that critiques the practice of violence in the interest of
neighborliness.[5]

Thus, the issue is joined in the narrative between the
imperial practice of extraction, commodity, and violence legitimated by the imperial gods, and the practice of neighborly
reality and fidelity legitimated by the emancipatory, covenant-making God of Israelite tradition. It is conventional to assign

to the imperial gods the qualities of omnipotence, omni-science, and omnipresence. And Yhwh, to be sure, is seen as well to be all-powerful, all-knowing, and everywhere present. These marks that are common among the gods, however, are not the most characteristic marking of Yhwh. In contrast to the gods of empire, Yhwh is praised and celebrated most char-acteristically for an eager capacity for fidelity. This turns out to be the tenacious, long-term commitment of Yhwh to Yhwh's covenant partners, Israel and all creation. It is fidelity that marks the good news of Israel's texts and that speaks broadly and passionately against extraction and commoditization.

The decisive difference in this God yields, derivatively, a decisively different notion of world history and of human persons in human community. When the gods are presented as legitimators of extraction and commoditization, then the mark of effective humanness is to be competent extractors who can reduce all else to dispensable commodity. When, however, the legitimating God is an agent of reliable, big-time fidelity, then the quintessence of humanness is the practice of such fidelity that embraces neighborliness and that eventu-ates in a society of public justice. Thus, in the emancipatory-covenantal tradition of the Old Testament, human agents are, in replication of the emancipatory, covenant-making God, charged with neighborly fidelity. Whereas imperial accounts of reality specialize in static order and the maintenance of pre-ferred arrangements in the political economy, the tradition of emancipatory covenant-making, by contrast, affirms human agents who have the capacity and responsibility to act trans-formatively for the well-being of the human community and the ecology of creation.

All of that pertains to the ancient context wherein the sub-versive narrative of Israel lived in ongoing tension with impe-rial accounts of reality, and amid that tension resisted imperial accounts while proposing alternatives. Our reading of these ancient texts is, characteristically, by way of analogue. We are drawn to trace out analogues between the "original" context of the text and our contemporary reading context. And when we do that, we find that we ourselves also read the biblical texts in contexts of imperial power.

While we can, in global context, identify other empires or would-be empires, closest to us are the imperial pretensions of the United States, for globalization is primarily a project of political economy propelled by the United States.[6] It is easy enough to see that the United States, with its inexhaustible consumerism, its unrivalled military power, and its growing economic gap between haves and have-nots, is a forceful, willful practitioner of extraction and commoditization.

In that context, our contemporary reading of the Bible, in its emancipatory, covenant-making trajectory, invites to sub-version, resistance, and alternative. In our present social circumstance of willful extraction and commoditization, the practice of neighborly fidelity, in replication of the neighborly fidelity of the God of the gospel, is a crucial mandate for the well-being of our society.

In the discussion that follows, I have taken "relationality" as the tag-word (hash-mark?) for neighborly fidelity that is situated in the narrative of emancipatory covenant-making. I have exposited that relationality in three themes:

- *Justice* of a distributive kind is the guarantee that every member of society can live in security, dignity, and well-being:

  > You must not distort justice; you must not show partiality; and you must not accept bribes, for a bribe blinds the eyes of the wise and subverts the cause of those who are in the right. Justice, and only justice, you shall pursue. (Deut 16:19-20)

  > For you tithe mint, dill, and cummin, and have neglected the weightier matters of the law: justice

and mercy and faith. It is these you ought to have
pursued without neglecting the others. (Matt 23:23)

Such justice precludes practices by which the powerful
can prey upon the vulnerable.

- *Grace* (mercy) is a generous reach beyond quid pro quo
assumptions in which the left-behind are abandoned
in despair and vulnerability. In the practice of extraction and commoditization, there is no chance for grace
that willingly violates the hard rules of privilege and
entitlement:

> The people who survived the sword
> found grace in the wilderness;
> When Israel sought for rest,
> the Lord appeared to him from far away. (Jer 31:2-3)

- *Law* is the guarantee of an ordered distribution of
social goods, social power, and social access that precludes extortion, abuse, and oppression against the
vulnerable. In a law-less political economy, as Fox Butterfield has seen with reference to the situation of Afri-
can Americans, the powerful are "above the law," and
the vulnerable are "outside the law," so that the law is
no protection.[7] In a law-full political economy, however, power and predation are not the decisive factors
in well-being, because law is or can be an organized,
legitimated form of neighborly fidelity.

Thus, the three themes that I have exposited—justice,
grace, and law—are shot through with neighborly fidelity (that
is legitimated by the emancipatory, covenant-making God of
Israel) that is to be performed in the human community that
is pledged to imitate this God. I have made my argument from
Old Testament texts; but it is amply clear that the same deep
commitment to neighborly fidelity occupies the New Testament church and the Christian tradition. Thus, Paul can write,
with a quote from Leviticus 19:18:

> For the whole law is summed up in a single commandment,
> "You shall love your neighbor as yourself." (Gal 5:14)

Imagine that: the whole law!!

There are no "neighbors" in the empire. There are only threats, allies of convenience, and dispensable labor. The Exodus–Sinai narrative is the normative emergence of "neighbor" in the history of the world. Imperial ideology has tried, forever and now, to eradicate that powerful emergent. For that reason, the issue has to be joined again and again, both between the anti-neighborly gods of the empire vis-à-vis the emancipatory, covenant-making God, and between their respective adherents, the human agents of extraction and commoditization and those who know themselves called to be agents of neighborly rehabilitation. My discussion is one such effort to join the issue in the ongoing contestation for the nature and quality of our shared future. This countertradition affirms that the world could be other than it is when managed by empires. It not only affirms that prospect; it energizes and empowers its adherents to be about that other way in the world that refuses imperial closure.

1

THE NATURE AND MISSION OF GOD
Irreducibly, Inscrutably Relational

A convergence of the themes of justice, grace, and law is a very tall order of immense complexity. Taken in biblical proportion, moreover, the convergence is notoriously elusive because of the impressionistic, almost playful way in which matters are rendered in narrative and poetic modes. The biblical evidence for such a convergence of themes takes in an enormous amount of material from many different perspectives over a long period of time. Any judgment rendered on the convergence is sure to be partial and provisional, but it is in any case our task.

I.

At the outset we must distinguish a biblical convergence of these themes from two quite influential perspectives. First, there is no doubt that Aristotle, with his rational analytic approach, continues to exercise important influence on our understanding of social power and social relationships. Aristotle is committed to a practice of fairness that would yield a peaceable community, but that fairness depends upon social differentiations that are taken as givens, differentiations that pertain to birth, property qualifications, and capabilities. The outcome, moreover, is a stratified society in which social harmony is established by assigning everyone to an appropriate social function and status.

Specifically, Aristotle's notion of justice is committed to the maintenance of order, with justice providing norms and sanctions to uphold stability. It is then inescapable that the term "justice" comes to be taken as retributive justice, a system of rewards and punishments for adherence to or violation of stable social harmony. There is no doubt that this is very different from the biblical perspective. There is, further, no doubt that the two perspectives, Aristotelian and biblical, are often confused or, better, innocently homogenized.

Second, Martin Luther broke decisively with Aristotle with his realization of the defining reality of God's grace, a dimension of social reality that is of course not present in Aristotle's reading. It is impossible to overstate the contribution of Luther to our evangelical understanding of these themes. But of course Luther came to his great insight with his great passion in his particular context. He could not have done otherwise. It turns out, however, that his deep distinction between gospel and law, so compelling in his context when law had become the performance of "works" prescribed by the church, has had significant influence in continuing ways. Part of that legacy is Reinhold Niebuhr's sharp distinction between "moral man" and "immoral society." In my Calvinist reading, such a way of formulating matters is difficult and deeply problematic, even if we want to affirm with Luther that the bottom, most elemental truth has to do with God's graciousness.

I propose that from a biblical, more particularly Old Testament perspective, we have a starting point that is very different from either Aristotle or Luther, though of course our familial linkage to Luther is much more immediate and compelling than that of Aristotle. In this presentation I want to consider a series of texts in turn, and from them I will reflect on themes that I believe are decisive for a biblical rendering of the convergence of justice, grace, and law. The beginning point for our consideration of justice, grace, and law is a relationship that is open, contested, ongoing in its dynamism, and life-or-death.

II.

I will begin with Hosea 2, an extended text that articulates the entire drama of relatedness that concerns justice, grace, and law. As you know, Hosea, in the eighth century when Israel was under threat from Assyria and when the socioeconomic infrastructure of society was unraveling, voiced his poetry according to the imagery of marriage that had emerged from his own life. Regularly, in critical judgment, Hosea either appealed to or helped to formulate the covenantal categories that were to be decisive for the prophetic tradition that was to follow, and for the crisis of exile that was to be durably definitional for Israel's faith and self-understanding. He is either a font or a way station in the dramatic articulation of what came to matter decisively in ancient Israel for justice, grace, and law.

David Clines has shown in detail how this chapter, in its final form, articulates a perfect rhetorical symmetry between the divorce suit (vv. 2-13) and the remarriage that opens the future for Israel (vv. 14-23).[1] The divorce that Yhwh declares against Israel is because of Israel's gross betrayal of covenantal fidelity, a deep affront to Yhwh. In this dramatic portrayal, at verse 14, Yhwh, the indignant wounded lover, abruptly reverses field. After issuing two "therefores" of harsh punishment, the poem pivots on a third "therefore." We expect a third statement of punishing indignation; but instead we get a new initiative offered without explanation. Yhwh proposes now to woo his fickle partner back to a relationship:

> Therefore, I will now allure her,
> and bring her into the wilderness,
> and speak tenderly to her.
> From there I will give her her vineyards,
> and make the Valley of Achor a door of hope.
> There she will respond as in the days of her youth,
> as at the time when she came out of the land of Egypt.
>
> (vv. 14-15)

The resolve of Yhwh is to transpose the Valley of Trouble (an allusion to a defeat in the book of Joshua) into a door of hope through which Israel may reenter the fecund land of promise. From that act that Yhwh does not doubt will be effective, Yhwh anticipates new futures of happy covenantal fidelity, of a renewed covenant with all creation including "the wild animals, birds of the air, and the creeping things of the ground," and a disarmament that will foster security.

And then, in the verses that will concern us, Yhwh voices a remarkable oath of fidelity that amounts to a wedding vow:

> And I will take you for my wife forever; I will take you for my wife in righteousness and in justice, in steadfast love, and in mercy. I will take you for my wife in faithfulness; and you shall know the Lord. (vv. 19-20)

1. This quite remarkable text provides the primary material out of which I want to explore our themes of justice, grace, and law. The terms of the restored relationship are five; I will propose (a) that this cluster of terms constitutes the primary data for our investigation and (b) that while each of these terms has its particular meaning, they all belong to the same semantic field and in sum they are all rough synonyms that provide a basis for our thinking.

Concerning these five terms:

- The first two, *mispat* and *sedeqah*, "justice and righteousness," constitute a recurring word pair that appears in the prophets, notably Amos and Isaiah, but also in Jeremiah. "Justice and righteousness" taken together are what we mean in our triad by "justice," the maintenance of a viable socioeconomic, political order that makes neighborly solidarity possible and available to all members of the community.

- The third term, *hesed*, "steadfast love," is commonly taken to mean covenantal fidelity, an engagement of relationality that requires long-term regard for and attentiveness to the other party. In such usage, this term is often linked to the fifth term, *amunah*, "faithfulness," so that this second pair yields a notion of reliable covenantal loyalty that is the foundation for justice and righteousness. Whereas "justice and righteousness" recur in the prophets as a defining mandate to Israel, the word pair "steadfast love and faithfulness" often occurs in doxologies that characterize Yhwh, most especially in Psalm 89 where the terms attest Yhwh's long-term commitment to David:

> My faithfulness and steadfast love shall be with him . . .
> But I will not remove from him my steadfast love,
> or be false to my faithfulness. (vv. 24, 33)

In Psalm 89:14, moreover, the four terms are given as pillars for the foundation of David's throne:

> Righteousness and justice are the foundation of
>   your throne;
> steadfast love and faithfulness are before you.

The close usage of the four terms, although they can be readily divided into two word pairs, shows the way in which all the terms concern the same matter of reliable, tenacious, transformative commitment that will sustain.

- The fourth term in the wedding vow of Hosea 2 is *raham*, "mercy." The term is used in Isaiah 49:15 as a wordplay with "womb," the same letters with different vowel pointing, so that Trible reads as "womb-like mother love."[2] The NRSV in Hosea 2 has "mercy," but it is elsewhere often rendered "compassion," so that of the five terms this one may be the most intimate and the most forceful concerning divine pathos and emotive commitment to Israel.

The five terms together, in something of a rhetorical torrent, witness to Yhwh's deep resolve on behalf of Israel. This divine resolve, moreover, comes in the wake of the deep wound and indignation of the preceding verses, so that the about-face made by Yhwh in verse 14 is given without warrant or explanation. That about-face is in the nature of Yhwh, and so it is defining for this relationship. Israel, so the poem attests, has done everything imaginable to escape this relationship for an easier, more manageable way in the world. But Yhwh tenaciously precludes such an escape. These are declarative statements in the vow by Yhwh that permit no thought of not being true!

Thus far the renewal is a unilateral imposition by Yhwh. It will be this way! It is only at the end of the vow that Yhwh adds: "You shall know the Lord." Of course the verb "know" is tricky, for it permits a wink toward "a biblical sense of knowing," and perhaps that sexual connotation is the measure of intimacy in the imagery. More likely, "know" means to acknowledge, recognize, and accept Yhwh's governance, as the term signifies in the Exodus narrative. That is, Israel will come to terms with the reality of fidelity in this intimate, demanding, imposed transformative relationship. That is a lot to "know"!

So now observe what happens through this poem. Hosea, we have no doubt, has in purview the socioeconomic crisis of Northern Israel. But he is an artist. He offers public reality troped by metaphor. Through the imaginative use of metaphor, he readily transposes social reality. After all, Hosea 2 is just a poem—if you like, an inspired poem, but just a poem. It is an artistic, imaginative rendering of a deep social crisis. In this imaginative, artistic rendering, the social crisis has been recharacterized in two ways: (a) It turns out that the crisis is not about nuts and bolts and jobs and tanks and bullets. It is about fidelity and betrayal and relational possibility. (b) It is not primarily about human agents who work their will, for now the public space is occupied by divine agency that lives in, with, and under political culture; history is reconceived and revisioned as an arena for this divine agent who extends fidelity and who summons to fidelity. In verse 18 it is imagined that disarmament and restored environment are the produce of covenantal fidelity. The poem ends in verses 21-23 with an anticipation of renewed creation. That is, God's resolve for the environment emerges through the practice of fidelity. It is the character of Yhwh who permits, in poetic imagination, the outcomes from relational terms . . . justice, righteousness, steadfast love, mercy, faithfulness. The poem posits from God's side a "knowing" commitment that overrides all other knowing, all of our "known knowns" and our "unknown knowns" and our "unknown unknowns." The horizon of social reality has been decisively rearticulated in ways that Aristotle could not have imagined, though Luther may have parsed it in this way. The outcome is a future that could not be derived from ancient reason. The poet has opened social possibility by sounding the note of tenacious fidelity that redefines everything.

2. If we read backward from Hosea 2 with attentiveness to that cluster of terms bespeaking fidelity, we will come finally to Exodus 34:6-7.[3] That text, apparently in God's own mouth but perhaps in the mouth of Moses, is a disclosure of Yhwh just after the alienation between Israel and Yhwh evoked by the bull (calf) of gold. Yhwh and Moses have been engaged in hard negotiation about the future in chapter 33. But then, in this magisterial utterance, the great terms of fidelity are again recited. Along with *hesed* (twice), *amunah*, and *raham*, we get in addition *hannan* (gracious), an idiom for "slow to anger," and

a particle, "forgiving." The new terms reinforce but do not basically alter the intent of the three terms that are familiar to us from the wedding vow in Hosea. The sum of the utterance is the readiness and capacity of Yhwh to engage Israel yet again, the affront of the calf notwithstanding. In this crisis as in Hosea, these terms give us what is most elemental and characteristic about Yhwh—namely, that Yhwh intends this relationship and will move past alienation to have it.

To be sure, there is an edge to this utterance; in verse 7 the statement is extended with an adversative "yet" that Yhwh will not acquit the guilty but visit retribution upon the coming generations. That brief statement has no exact counterpart in Hosea 2, except that the divorce proceedings in Hosea 2:2-13 sound the same note: violation of the relationship and its norms of fidelity are taken with utmost seriousness. Thus, I judge that the same counterpoint is present here; only here the negative comes second, whereas in Hosea the negative is followed by the positive of restoration and renewal.

The narrative outcome of this utterance, following the negative, is that Moses must offer a passionate imperative petition to Yhwh for "pardon" (34:9). And in verse 10, Yhwh concedes the point and resolves to renew the covenant relationship that has been violated:

> I hereby make a covenant. Before all your people I will perform marvels, such as have not been performed in all the earth in any nation; and all the people among whom you live shall see the work of the Lord; for it is an awesome thing that I will do with you. (v. 10)

The new action now promised by Yhwh concerns "marvels" (wonders). The promise makes clear that what comes as renewal is nothing ordinary; it is a self-giving that is spectacular and underived. As in Hosea 2, the future possibility, in the face of alienation, comes from a new initiative by this God who will have this relationship.

3. If we read forward from Hosea 2, again with attentiveness to our cluster of terms, we will come to the remarkable assertion in Lamentations 3:22-23. The statement is remarkable because it occurs amid the five long laments over failed Jerusalem. In that body of lament, these verses are the only utterance of new possibility. In the midst of the third lament, the speaker voices the loss of hope that is experienced in the savaging of the city:

> My soul is bereft of peace;
> I have forgotten what happiness is;
> so I say, "Gone is my glory,
> and all that I had hoped for from the Lord."
> The thought of my affliction and my homelessness is worm-
>   wood and gall!
> My soul continually thinks of it and is bowed down within me.
>   (vv. 17-20)

Gone is glory! Gone is hope! Gone is possible future!

But of course this poem is remembered and preserved because that departure of hope is not the final word. The lament continues in a most characteristic line of Israel's reasoning:

> But this I call to mind,
> And therefore I have hope. (v. 21)

Israel may despair; but it refuses amnesia. What it recalls is the great cluster of terms for fidelity, each of which is embedded in a particular narrative possibility. The speaker can recall the very divine wonders that were promised in the renewal of Exodus 34:10. The wonders here are not spectacles of strength and power. They are rather manifestations of fidelity that linger in the abyss:

> The steadfast love of the Lord never ceases,
> his mercies never come to an end;
> they are new every morning;
> great is your faithfulness. (vv. 22-23)

We get three of our terms from the vow in Hosea that are also sounded post-calf in Exodus: *hesed, raham* (plural), and *amunah*. In its season of bereftment, without evidence of divine attentiveness, Israel survives in despair by the capacity to remember, recite, and take seriously. What is remembered, recited, and taken seriously are covenant fidelity, compassion, and reliability. The outcome of such remembering is this stunning "therefore," as a result, "I hope!" This is a most Jewish transaction. The action of remembering fidelity permits anticipation of coming fidelity.

By the end of this particular lament in chapter 3, the speaker can affirm that "from the depths of the pit" I called (v. 55). God came near:

> You came near when I called on you;
> you said, "Do not fear!" (v. 57)

In verses 58-61 we get a vigorous affirmation of Yhwh's attentiveness:

> You have taken up my cause, O Lord,
> you have redeemed my life.
> You have seen the wrong done to me, O Lord;
> judge my cause.
> You have seen all their malice,
> all their plots against me.
> You have heard their taunts, O Lord,
> all their plots against me.

And then a series of petitions that do not doubt divine attentiveness:

> Pay them back for their deeds, O Lord,
> according to the work of their hands!
> Give them anguish of heart;
> your curse be on them!
> Pursue them in anger and destroy them
> from under the Lord's heavens. (vv. 64-66)

Everything depends on a remembering of past divine fidelity that is the basis for new possibility. This remembered fidelity levels the field, against great odds, for expectation and vindication.

4. I will cite one other cluster of our terms in Psalm 85. This text cannot be dated and is something of an outlier. It begins in a series of affirmations about Yhwh's good attentiveness (vv. 1-3), followed by an insistent petition:

> Restore us, again, O God our salvation,
> and put away your indignation toward us . . .
> Show us your salvation, O Lord,
> and grant us your salvation. (vv. 4, 7)

The petition is sandwiched at the beginning and the end by "salvation": "our salvation" in verse 4, "your salvation" in verse 7.

But then in verses 10-13 we get a very different kind of rhetoric that yet again voices the cluster of terms that preoccupy us:

> Steadfast love and faithfulness will meet;
> righteousness and peace will kiss each other.
> Faithfulness will spring up from the ground,
> and righteousness will look down from the sky. (vv. 10-11)

We get *hesed, amunah* (twice), *sedeqah* (twice), supplemented by *shalom*, which we can now incorporate into our cluster of defining terms. The whole is quite remarkable, suggesting that steadfast love, faithfulness, *shalom*, and righteousness are cosmic forces or active agents that engage each other. The poem can imagine a stunning convergence of all of these forces of well-being that will comprehend ground and sky, heaven and earth.

The outcome of a fidelity-saturated creation is that Yhwh, the creator and the initiator of fidelity, will "give" in a way that causes fruitful abundance:

> The Lord will give what is good,
> and our land will yield its increase. (v. 12)

The creator long since has called creation "very good." What makes it "very good" is the faithful "meeting and kissing" of all of its elements in an exhibit of generative solidarity. The way to environmental health is through fidelity! The psalm concludes with yet a third reiteration of righteousness:

> Righteousness will go before him,
> and will make a path for his steps. (v. 13)

The imagery presents the creation as a life-giving enterprise that becomes a path of righteousness that even Yhwh may walk.

Thus, the outcome of "meeting and kissing" in Psalm 85 is a counterpart to the outcome of the new covenantal marriage of Hosea 2:19-20. This view of fidelity concerns specifically Yhwh and Israel. But Hosea knows that the work of that relationship has immense implications for generativity that reach beyond Israel to the well-functioning of creation:

> I will answer the heavens and they shall answer the earth;
> and the earth shall answer the grain, the wine, and the oil,
> and they shall answer Jezreel;
> and I will sow him for myself in the land.
> And I will have pity on Lo-ru-hamah,
> And I will say to Lo-ammi,
> "You are my people";
> and he shall say, "You are my God." (2:21-23)

It is all about "answering." It concerns engagement with and response to. The poem imagines God (creator), heavens, earth, grain, wine, oil, sowing, all in generative sync. And finally, in the wake of a restored creation, comes a restored Israel in this perfect covenantal symmetry: "You are my people / You are my God"!

III.

I take these four texts as representative and typical articulations of the imaginative ways of justice, grace, and law on the horizon of the Old Testament:

Hosea 2:2-23—concerning alienation and reconciliation;

Exodus 34:6-7—concerning violated covenant and restored covenant;

Lamentations 3:20-22—concerning lost hope and recovered hope; and

Psalm 85:10-13—imagining restoration beyond anger.

One could quibble about whether other texts would do better than the ones I have selected, or whether I have heard these texts faithfully. But one cannot dispute the fact that a recurring validation and confirmation of fidelity provides the primary insight for our work. That vocabulary of fidelity is resistant to technical or instrumental reason, to positive law, to authoritarian settlement, and to many of the temptations and distortions that beset our public life. Thus, in sum, the truth of our life is as an ongoing, interactive drama that remains open-ended, subject to repair, and grounded in generosity. That much is given in this recurring vocabulary that makes the unmistakable claim that at bottom, reality is interactive and does not permit settled closure. From that I deduce the following:

1. Life is all about interactive relationships. This claim goes very far in resisting claims of essentialism, because the outworking of the tradition is not in settled formulations of ontology but in ongoing dramatic performances in which the players maintain some constancy of character but are endlessly open to surprise disputation, reversal, and fresh initiative. Such a way of discerning reality flies in the face of much settled opinion in Western culture and, consequently, in the face of much settled opinion about theological truth and about the character of public political life.

It is this commitment to relationality that makes the Old Testament peculiar, that has over time made Jewish modes of thought and interpretation such an inexplicable presence in our common life, an inexplicable reality that is taken too often as a threat to be feared or as a misfit to be expelled. It is, more-over, an inescapable reality to which the church is variously and awkwardly an heir.

This commitment to relationality is, in the text, irreducible. It cannot be transposed into anything else, try as we might. We frequently wish for something less risky or less vexing or less demanding, and so we try to transpose this relationality into formula or syllogism or creed, but we cannot. We try to reduce it by freezing God into attributes, and we try to categorize human essences. All our freezing and categorizing, however, turn out to be feeble in the face of the vitality and insistence of this defining and defying relationality that continues to summon us.

This commitment to relationality is inscrutable, because it defies all of our categories of explanation. The actual testimony to the God who indwells this tradition depicts a strangely unsettling character. We smooth out the testimony for purposes of credibility and coherence, but what we are given is a God with a full range of emotional capacity, whose name is revealed and yet enigmatic, who makes promises of presence and is experienced as absent, who is self-giving but who has an exaggerated sense of self-regard, who presides over all but who picks and accompanies favorites, who meets and comforts and yet remains hidden.

The human counterpart in this interaction is equally inscrutable. How could we not be, since we take our life from that source? We are, we human creatures, a deep enigma to ourselves. We are dazzled and baffled that we are fearfully and wonderfully made (Ps 139:14).[4] And long before Romans 7, we have come to understand that we are multivoiced, multilayered creatures filled with ambiguity and contradiction, capable of insatiable self-regard, deeply needy and profoundly inadequate, and yet capable of profound generosity and risk. It is all right to make it doxological about us with the psalmist: "What is man?" (Ps 8:4). "What is humankind?" But then, in honesty, we know the truth is not found only in doxological dazzlement, but can as well require bottomless liturgies of dismay.

The inexplicable human creatures made for relationships are mandated, since Jubal and Tubal-cain, to make tools, to imagine cities, and to form societies (Gen 4:21-22). And we do make and imagine and form. But such cities and societies are formed by creatures like us, filled with ambiguity, destined for interaction, ambiguous at best and resistant at worst to the ways we must form and inhabit. As a result, we imagine neighborhoods filled with neighbors, always to discover that the neighbors are as acutely unsettled as are we. Our habitations are promise-filled and vexatious, resolved for fidelity but most often fidelity-distorted and unembraced.

2. The parties to this relationality—God, self, and the neighbor—are variously called to fidelity in our irreducible, inscrutable relationality. All the vocabulary I have traced attests to the defining importance of fidelity. It is the deepest mark of the sponsoring, legitimating God. It is the deepest affirmation of human agents who depend upon fidelity for life, without which there is only alienation and despair. The tradition traces the marks of fidelity.

(a) Fidelity requires direct face-to-face address that sounds like oath-taking. Direct speech is the medium of fidelity. I am struck, are you not, that the substantive realities of public life depend upon the maintenance of venues for face-to-faceness. Thus a court of law where public life is adjudicated depends on utterance under oath, oath that vouches for reliable truth-telling. Or alternatively, even in a secular culture, the altar is still the vow-taking place for naming, for marrying, for the closures of death, and even for the routines of forgiveness that make public life possible: "I announce and declare to you that your sins are forgiven." The one who administers the oath and validates the promises is one taken to have a transcendent authority that guarantees the truth. In ancient Israel, it was before the altar that one was sometimes said to be "before God."

(b) Fidelity entails making and keeping promises. It requires commitments of reliability into unforeseen futures. Thus, the remarriage of Hosea 2 is pervaded by promises, even though neither party could know at the moment of utterance what that might mean:

> I will have pity on Lo-ru-hamah
> and I will say to Lo-ammi,
> "You are my people,"
> and he shall say, "You are my God." (v. 23)

That covenant formula, repeatedly voiced in Jeremiah and Ezekiel, became the ground for getting through the exilic displacement when all easier guarantees had failed.[5] It is reminiscent of the solemn, formal, and symmetrical oaths of covenant in Deuteronomy 26:17-19:

> Today you have obtained the Lord's agreement: to be your God; and for you to walk in his ways, to keep his statutes, his commandments, and his ordinances, and to obey him. Today the Lord has obtained your agreement: to be his treasured people, as he promised you, and to keep his commandments; for him to set you high above all nations that he has made, in praise and in fame and in honor; and for you to be a people holy to the Lord your God, as he promised you.

Indeed, the entire project begins in the trustworthy promise that Abraham trusted:

> I will make of you a great nation, and I will bless you, and make your name great, so that you will be a blessing. (Gen 12:2)

And finally Israel responded at Sinai with an oath concerning the commandments:

> All that the Lord has spoken we will do, and we will be obedient. (Exod 24:7; see v. 3)

The promise made to Abraham concerned land, people, dynasty, state, and a long-vexed companionship; it turned out that Israel's responding vow of allegiance eventuated in a passionate commitment to Torah that placed Israel in contradiction to the usual suspects of wealth, power, and control. It turned out, as in every oath of fidelity, that futures are more costly than anyone could know ahead of time. But promises are to be kept, for promises generate the neighborhood.

(c) Fidelity pertains to the common good, a prospect that pertains to all parties. The common good goes under the banner of *shalom*. Israel's fidelity is to God's *shalom*, to "trust and obey," for there is no other way to be happy or to engage in the pursuit of happiness. It turned out that Yhwh's part in the common good is to provide safety and food, to generate the elemental sustenance that Israel could not generate for itself. It turned out, perhaps to the surprise of both parties, that the common good requires investment in the neighborhood, and attentiveness to the neighbors, most particularly the neighbor left vulnerable, unprotected, and in need. The common good of *shalom* means that none can be excluded or disregarded, none can be left behind, not the widow, not the orphan, not the immigrant. The common good means that Yhwh is not free to go off to God's own self but commonly summoned to care about the rest of us. It also means that no member of this narrative of fidelity is free to seek a self-indulgent well-being; all are summoned back to the reality of the community.

(d) That common good is expressed as bodily *shalom*. It is elemental to the Old Testament that the familiar words for fidelity . . . *hesed, amunah, raham, mispat, sedeqah* . . . can never be tilted toward the simply "spiritual," but are always concerned with the political, social, bodily well-being of all the members of the body politic. The line that runs from creation to covenant to incarnation is a line of materiality. The data of fidelity concern land, crops, houses, and fields that are vehicles for God's faithful blessing. Fidelity concerns flourishing materiality:

> Blessed shall you be in the city, and blessed shall you be in the field.
> Blessed shall be the fruit of your womb, the fruit of your ground, and the fruit of your livestock, both the increase of your cattle and the issue of your flock.
> Blessed shall be your basket and your kneading bowl.
> Blessed shall you be when you come in, and blessed shall you be when you go out. (Deut 28:3-6)

The blessing pertains to nothing less than every element of life in the neighborhood:

> ... city and field ... urban life and agriculture;
> ... fruit of your womb, your ground, your livestock, your cattle, your flock, your means of production, your capacity for sustenance;
> ... blessed basket and kneading bowl, mundane domesticity;
> ... going out and coming in, the rhythm of the day, of work and rest, perhaps the reality of war, going out to risk and coming home to safety.

"Blessed, blessed, blessed, blessed, blessed," the coinage of the common experience of the body politic infused with the holy force of life.

(e) Fidelity is grounded in unmocked holiness. This is a God before whom shoes are taken off. This is a God whose mountain is dangerous, to be kept holy. There is nothing easy or casual about this mutuality. The result is a guarantee about this interaction that must not be presumed upon. From that it follows that Israel, in this relationship, is not free to shape the forbidding summons of God into something that we like better—that is, Israel is not free for graven images, not free for commoditization, not free for idols. The critical function of that divine holiness is to render all other efforts at the common good penultimate and at best provisional. This reality warns against absolutizing any public arrangement by class, race, gender, ideology, national state, ecclesial phrase or edifice. This ultimacy calls out every serious penultimacy, as serious as it may be, as always penultimate, open to revision and reformulation.

Nowhere is it said in the tradition that the neighbor is holy. But it does say, "Be Holy." All of you be holy. All of you be holy because the Lord your God is holy. I expect none of us would vote for every proposal in the book of Leviticus; we pick and choose. But the teaching of the holiness tradition is not in this or that rule; rather, the intent of the holiness tradition, taken in sum, is to fend off the reduction of public life into profanation that fails to respect, honor, or take seriously the deep mystery of the public good and the neighbors who inhabit it. When profanation is unchecked by a resolve to holiness, life becomes cheap, neighbors become dispensable, and the common good becomes subject to cynical distortion. In its practice of fidelity, Israel knew that the formation and maintenance of the common good was not simply an accident or a convenience. It was rather a common task. And the relentless reflection of the prophets is that this vocation of the common good had not been honored or taken seriously.

Ezekiel is the rawest voice in characterizing what happens when the common life is reduced to pornographic dimensions. It is undone and dismantled precisely because the Lord of the relationship will not be mocked. That profanation is not simply the affront of lurid, explicit visuals but the pornography of torture, of hunger amid affluence, of exploitation amid prosperity, of drones, and of the cynical power of the haves against the have-nots. This urgent summons to holiness will not only watch as glory departs the temple, but can say of the scandal of Sodom:

> This was the guilt of your sister Sodom: she and her daughters had pride, excess of food, and prosperous ease, but did

not aid the poor and needy. They were haughty and did abominable things before me. (16:49-50)

Talk about holiness!

(f) Fidelity is relentless in what coach Bud Wilkinson used to call "second effort." Coach Wilkinson loved to talk about a halfback who was completely blocked, but who could spin around, go free, and gain yards. Fidelity is about second effort. So God promises covenantal fidelity after the golden calf. So Yhwh makes new wedding vows after the indignation and shame of broken marriage. So the voice of Lamentations will hope in God's fidelity after the failure of Jerusalem. Fidelity is the resolve of loyalty that is undeterred and unimpeded by the most unbearable of circumstances. Whatever we may say subsequently about our triad of justice, grace, and law is to be said in the context of that fidelity.

3. Relationships require divine agency. Israel's tradition of reliability depends completely upon attesting to Yhwh as a real character and active agent in the life of the world.[6] The text of course does that with confidence, but there were, even in ancient days, detractors from such a claim. They did not deny God; they denied God's agency:

> In the pride of their countenance the wicked say, "God will not
>   seek it out";
> all their thoughts are, "There is no God." . . .
> They think in their heart, "God has forgotten,
> he has hidden his face, he will never see it." (Ps 10:4, 11)

> Fools say in their hearts, "There is no God."
> They are corrupt, they do abominable deeds;
> there is no one who does good. (Ps 14:1)

> And they say, "How can God know?
> Is there knowledge in the Most High?" (Ps 73:11)

> They have spoken falsely of the Lord,
> and have said, "He will do nothing.

No evil will come upon us,
and we shall not see sword or famine." (Jer 5:12)

I will punish . . . those who say in their hearts,
"The Lord will not do good,
nor will he do harm." (Zeph 1:12)

It is characteristically the powerful and the affluent—that is, the autonomous—who dare the claim. Of course the claim is even more acute among us, given our Enlightenment circumstance. So Douglas Ottati, for example, can judge that trust in divine agency is "hypernaturalism."[7] We appeal to a dozen euphemisms to get around the embarrassment. But of course the tradition, in its primary articulation, was not embarrassed.[8] It knew that the story could not be told without agency.

(a) God as agent is said both to set limits on practices that are prohibited and to summon to practices that are commended. Thus Jeremiah can have God say:

Do you not fear me? Says the Lord;
Do you not tremble before me?
I placed the sand as a boundary for the sea,
a perpetual barrier that it cannot pass;
though the waves toss, they cannot prevail,
though they roar, they cannot pass over it. (5:22)

The poem goes on from a meditation on creation to reflect on rapacious economics in which no boundary is observed:

Like a cage full of birds,
their houses are full of treachery;
therefore they have become great and rich,
they have grown fat and sleek.
They know no limits in deeds of wickedness;
they do not judge with justice the cause of the orphan, to make
it prosper,
and they do not defend the rights of the needy. (vv. 27-28)

No limits! A contrast to the limit of the seashore as a perpetual barrier. It is this divinely set limit in the fabric of creation that grounds the common good that is repeatedly sounded in the Decalogue: Thou shalt not . . . not . . . not . . . not. Of course, such a limit can be formulated as an impersonal linkage between deeds and consequences. But within the covenant tradition, the link of deeds to consequences is made by the God who acts as adjudicating agent.

(b) God as agent is said to be endlessly available and attentive to other parties in the relationship. The entire prayer life of "call . . . answer" that Claus Westermann has shown to be central to the tradition is an exhibit of the way in which this God is attentive to the needs of the partners.[9] Of course it did not always work out that way. Much of the prayer life of Israel, in the Psalms, consists of a recognition that God is not attentive and available. It is the assumption of such prayers, however, that Israel has a great entitlement to such divine availability and attentiveness, even if God is abusive and neglectful, and has, for a time, reneged on fidelity. Beyond that insistent recognition, however, is the remarkable attestation that the summons of Israel does indeed evoke the presence of Yhwh. Yhwh is on call, perhaps reluctantly on call, but on call. In the immediate crisis in the text, Yhwh can even concede an instant of abandonment:

> For a brief moment I abandoned you,
> but with great compassion I will gather you.
> In overflowing wrath for a moment
> I hid my face from you,
> but with everlasting love I will have compassion on you,
> says the Lord, your Redeemer. (Isa 54:7-8)

That concession, however, is stated in order to articulate the new resolve of abiding, durable, compassionate attentiveness. And finally, the divine assurance is:

> Before they call I will answer,
> while they are yet speaking I will hear. (Isa 65:24)

Thus will fidelity finally be kept!

(c) Agency carries with it transformative potential and capacity. Yhwh's fidelity is not only presence or attentiveness. It is presence that performs and attentiveness that alters circumstance. Thus, the "comfort" of Second Isaiah is not just handholding; it is homecoming in defiance of the Babylonian Empire. Thus, "agency" in this relationship is a dynamic intrusion in order that renewal, transformation, and restoration may be the order of the day. That agency is future-generating.

4. Now I think that divine agency is hard enough. For our purposes, however, what is even harder is human agency. With the loss of the common good, the nullification of "society" by Margaret Thatcher, and the epidemic of privatization all around us, the notion of human agency in the public domain is in retreat. Better, safer, and more profitable to confine one's energy to control and moneymaking at the expense of the common good. Or better yet to participate in the common good in order to acquire money and control. The idea of agency in the service of the common good in order to serve the common good has become an oddity in a society that is long on commodity and short on reliability.

But of course, the irreducible, inscrutable relationality of the tradition summons not only God as agent but human agents as well. The core human vocation, in imitation of God, is to be a guarantor, maintainer, and generator of the common good.[10] We may, I suggest, take the three dimensions of agency that I have identified for God and see them as marks for human agency in this relationship.

(a) Human agents may set limits on chaos as did the creator God. Social chaos arises when the vulnerable are left undefended and exposed to the confiscatory propensity of, as Jeremiah calls them, "scoundrels." And we know a great deal about the chaos of racism! Limits must be set. The force of chaos must be restrained. In a small face-to-face community, this may be done by custom and social expectation. In more complex ordering, it requires regulation and forcible restraint that can be enacted only by human agents. Thus, the common good requires not only the blessing and legitimacy of divine agency but the investment of human agents.

(b) Human agents may practice availability for and attentiveness to the public process. We may, like God, be sometimes AWOL. But constant and sustained participation in the public process belongs to human relationality.

(c) Human agents, like the divine agent, have a capacity for transformative action. Thus, in context, the human person is defined as a neighborhood-generating actor. That role has been the case since the time of Moses. In Exodus 3 the God of the bush makes extravagant, rather flamboyant promises to Israel. But then Yhwh reverses field and says to Moses, "You go to Pharaoh." Exodus emancipation is a human project. The common good, so the tradition attests, requires divine resolve and legitimation, and bold human agency. Indeed, the prophetic strictures may be seen as rebukes to those who had the capacity for societal generativity but who had dropped out of that role in the service of self-interest. Human agency in this relationship is characteristically in a readiness, as Paul asserts, to

> look not to your own interests, but to the interests of others. (Phil 2:4)

5. Relationality means to look to the interests of others. It belongs to the character of this God to look after the interests of others.[11] In broadest terms the other turns out to be creation. By the initial act of blessing of creation, God has transmitted and entrusted to creation as other the capacity for life and fruitfulness. In quite specific terms, the other who constitutes God's defining partner is Israel. The act of choosing, of "setting God's heart on," is a performed commitment to the well-being of the other. Taken in a form extrapolated from the choosing of Israel, God's preferential option for the

poor is a matter of taking the vulnerable and the resource-less as the other. In all three cases—creation, Israel, and the poor—God's own self-sufficiency and self-preoccupation are radically modified. The God of the Bible is primarily preoccupied not with God's own well-being but with an interaction that evokes the well-being of the other and yields for God unending doxology.

This reach toward the other does not constitute an abandonment of self. Clearly the God who extends self on behalf of the other has an acute sense of self-regard. At its best, God's self-regard and God's regard for the other converge. But we must not be romantic about that convergence, because there is clearly evidence that God's self-regard sometimes prevails over regard for the other, occasions that are performed as "judgment" when the other has not seriously regarded God's own self. This two-sided matter of self-regard and regard for the other is not reducible to a formula but endlessly under negotiation.

6. Derivatively, the summons to God's chosen people is to reach toward the other. Indeed, "othering" is a vocation that tells deeply about Israel's life in the world. We may identify three "others" who keep appearing in Israel's life, others who are acknowledged to be in the sphere of God's governance:

(a) The other who lives under the aegis of God's governance includes widow, orphan, and immigrant. The reach of Israel is an economic reach that interrupts and inconveniences the self-preoccupation of the chosen. In Deuteronomy 10:18 it is asserted that Yhwh "loves the stranger (immigrant)." It follows that it is a mandate to Israel "to love the stranger, for you were strangers in the land of Egypt."

(b) Eunuchs and foreigners embody a threatening other that Israel is inclined to repel by its purity codes. Thus, especially in Isaiah 56, a text that struggles against exclusion moves to the large affirmation that "my house shall be called a house of prayer for all peoples" (Isa 56:7).

(c) Israel is endlessly engaged in adjudication about the status of other peoples/states in a world of Yhwh's rule. Patrick Miller has observed how the early chapters of Deuteronomy take into account kinship with other peoples who have a legitimate claim of their own that Israel must recognize and honor:

> The Lord's stories with other peoples are made a part of Israel's story.[12]

And at the edge of the Old Testament, the poetry can even imagine that God has many chosen peoples:

> On that day Israel will be the third with Egypt and Assyria, a blessing in the midst of the earth, whom the Lord of hosts has blessed, saying: "Blessed be Egypt my people, and Assyria the work of my hands, and Israel my heritage." (Isa 19:24-25)

The poetry takes up God's pet names for Israel and generously assigns them across the Near East to Israel's long-term adversaries. The reach of the text is God's own reach, but God's reach clearly has implications for the reach of Israel.

When we look beyond the Old Testament, moreover, we are bound to see that the church's bold opening to Gentiles under the impetus of Peter's trance and Paul's testimony is the most extreme case of othering, an othering that decisively redefines the terms of fidelity and the character of the host people who "other." It is no wonder that Paul can say of this decision that the promise to the nations via Abraham was indeed "the gospel beforehand" (Gal 3:8), because this is a relentless reach of othering that is constitutive of Israel's vocation as God's chosen. This is, of course, rooted in the tradition of Abraham; but it is surprisingly so as well in the Sinai tradition, in which Israel as chosen is to be a "priestly kingdom" with a vocation vis-à-vis other kingdoms.

For that reason, Paul can offer an amazing hermeneutical statement about God's reach:

As it is written,

"Therefore I will confess you among the Gentiles,
And sing praises to your name";

and again he says,

"Rejoice, O Gentiles, with his people";

and again,

"Praise the Lord, all you Gentiles,
And let all the peoples praise him";

and again Isaiah says,

"The root of Jesse shall come,
the one who rises to rule the Gentiles;
in him the Gentiles shall hope." (Rom 15:9-12)

Along with allusion to Abraham, this text consists in quotes from the Old Testament (LXX) with Paul's accent on the Gentiles. The result is that Gentiles join the doxology to God and are invited into joy. The outcome of such a lyrical risk is a firm resistance to every exclusionary rule, every easy selection of traditions, and every preoccupation with self and self's own kind.

I will of course return to this. For now, however, I cite the remarkable statement of Martha Nussbaum. She has entitled her study of Hindu-Muslim relations in India *The Clash Within*. She intends by her title to engage Samuel Huntington and his older thesis of a coming and inevitable clash between the West and Islam. Against that claim, Nussbaum proposes that the "clash" is not between great theological-cultural traditions. It is, she writes, rather a clash within each of us, hence the title of her book:

The real "clash of civilizations" is not "out there," between admirable Westerners and Muslim zealots. It is here, within each person, as we oscillate uneasily between self-protective aggression and the ability to live in the world with others.[13]

And of course we may see that same clash within the text, where the struggle for the other and against the other is pervasive. There may be ground against the other, but it will not be found in the radical teaching of fidelity that draws the other into the orbit of fidelity. It is evident in every case—with God, with Israel, with the church—that the reach to the other, the ultimate fidelity, is a reach that redefines the reacher. So God, in a reach beyond self to creation, to Israel, to the poor, becomes a different God. So Israel, in its reach toward widows, orphans, and immigrants, becomes a different kind of chosen people. So the church, in its Spirit-led reach to Gentiles, becomes a different kind of community. It is not, "To thine own self be true." It is rather, "To the farthest reach of the other, be true."

7. I finish by adding one note that arises from the reach of fidelity to the other. In Hosea 2:21-23, the new vows of fidelity by the wounded, indignant lover lead, in the final verses, to an expectation about the fruitfulness of creation that in turn concerns the renewal of covenant between Yhwh and Israel:

> I will answer the heavens and [the heavens] shall answer
>   the earth;
> and the earth shall answer the grain, the wine, and the oil,
> and they shall answer Jezreel;
> and I will sow him for myself in the land.
> And I will have pity on Lo-ru-hamah,
> And I will say to Lo-ammi,
> "You are my people";
> and he shall say, "You are my God."

In Psalm 85:12-13, after the collage of meeting and kissing, the outcome is:

> Yhwh will give what is good,
> and our land will yield its increase.

Thus, the embrace of faithfulness from the ground and righteousness from the sky, from the two great zones of creation, results in agricultural flourishing.

The culmination of both Hosea 2:21-23 and Psalm 85:12-13 is restored, renewed, fruitful, flourishing creation. Relationality, in largest scope, concerns the character and the future of the whole of creation. It is as though these texts anticipate the plentitude of the new creation voiced in Ephesians and Colossians.

As pertains to our themes of justice, grace, and law, the matter is made clear in the two as yet untranslated books of Hans Heinrich Schmid.[14] The bold thesis of Schmid is given in one of his titles, *Gerechtigkeit als Weltordnung*, "righteousness as world order." As far as I know, Schmid has only one article translated into English that summarizes his work; it has been further elucidated in the Old Testament theology of Rolf Knierim.[15] Schmid's thesis is that *sedeqah*, one of our five terms, is not only about human morality or obedience; it concerns the way in which God has ordered and governs the earth as a life-giving, life-nourishing, life-sustaining relationship. Thus, the relationality is as large and comprehensive as we are able to imagine.

And because we are given, in the text, relationality that concerns the one who lingers in faithfulness, this means there is no final reading, no final solution, no grand theory, no master explanation. What we are given, rather, is a field of negotiation and adjudication. In that open field, Yhwh and Yhwh's other—creation, Israel, church—are summoned to the practice of faithful freedom that is risky and costly. The whole of the tradition is a meditation on God's risky freedom in seeking out partners who are called to a consummate kind of freedom, the freedom of agency in response. Imagine that othering in freedom! Righteousness and peace will kiss each other (Ps 85:10)! It is a kiss that is laden with and generative of new possibilities that are unexpected and inexplicable until that moment of cosmic fidelity.

We come to our work on justice, grace, and law, then, with an angle of vision remote from Aristotle:

- It arises from our meditation on the five big verbs of renewal.
- It is all about relationship.
- Risky lingering is the order of every day.
- It requires agency in freedom.
- It reaches beyond every comfort zone to the other.

In the end, such relationality trumps our preferred order with new possibility.

2

JUSTICE
From Zion Back to Sinai

Jacques Derrida, in his exposition of "the force of law," writes,

> Justice in itself, if such a thing exists . . . is not decon-structible. No more than deconstruction, if such a thing exists. Deconstruction is justice.[1]

This dictum of Derrida is part of his enigmatic program of deconstruction. But it is also a provisional acknowledgment of the limit of deconstruction. Justice is deconstruction of all else. It is clear to me, moreover, that Derrida's statement is not only part of his program. It is a thoroughly Jewish claim. In the Jewish tradition wrought from the Hebrew Bible, justice is beyond deconstruction, a non-negotiable given ordered in the structure of creation by the will of the creator God, Yhwh. What is endlessly to be deconstructed are all claims to truth that legitimate injustice. If we take justice to be economic vali-dation of the neighbor for the sake of the common good, we are remote from all positive law and from all ideological cant that serves as truth in the halls of power. In this presenta-tion I will consider the big public claims of justice in the Old

Testament, and then push behind and beneath those claims to the sources of urgency and adrenaline that make justice undeconstructible.

I.

A beginning point is to notice the ease and readiness with which the liturgies of Zion commit to justice. If we allow for Mowinckel's hypothesis of an enthronement festival that dominated and defined the worship in the Jerusalem temple, we can see that the psalms of enthronement celebrate and enact the right ordering of creation and so the right ordering of social power as well.[2] That right ordering by Yhwh, creator of heaven and earth, entails the defeat of the other gods, idols who are perpetrators of chaos:

> He has established the world;
> it shall never be moved. (Ps 93:1)

Justice is linked to the maintenance of a viable ordering of common life. That right ordering assures stability:

> The world is firmly established; it shall never be moved.
> He will judge (*spt*) the peoples with equity . . .
> For he is coming to judge (*spt*) the earth.
> He will judge (*spt*) the world with righteousness (*sedeqah*)
> and the peoples with his truth (*amunah*). (96:10, 13)

This doxology utilizes the term *shaphat* three times, the same root as *mispat* (justice). This is the lord of justice!

> Righteousness and justice are the foundation of his throne. . . .
> The heavens proclaim his righteousness . . .
> Zion hears and is glad . . .
> because of your judgments (*mispat*), O God . . .
> Light dawns for the righteous (*sedeqah*)
> and joy for the upright in heart. (97:2, 6, 8, 11)

> He has remembered his steadfast love (*hesed*) and faithfulness (*emeth*) to the house of Israel. All the ends of the earth have seen the victory of our God. . . .

He is coming to judge (*spt*) the earth.
He will judge (*spt*) the world with righteousness (*sedeqah*),
and the peoples with his equity. (98:3, 9)

Mighty king, lover of justice (*mispat*),
you have established equity;
you have executed justice (*mispat*) and righteousness (*sedeqah*) in
Jacob. (99:4)

Following Mowinckel, I have suggested previously that this liturgical performance is an act of construction of social reality (like all liturgy) in which the world is performed as a venue for justice that is guaranteed by the king as judge.[3] It is important that the noun "justice" (*mispat*) and the verb "judge" (*shaphat*) are in Hebrew the same word, so that divine judgment is the implementation and guarantee of justice.

It will be clear that these psalms conform exactly to the proposal of Hans Heinrich Schmid in *Gerechtigkeit als Weltordnung*.[4] The work of creation, liturgy by liturgy, is to order the world for righteousness. But the world ordered as righteousness is not an already guaranteed given. It is rather the outcome of Yhwh's work that is done now in liturgic imagination. It is work always again to be performed. That regularly performed liturgical work indicates that justice in the world is not assured. It depends on intense attentiveness from the judge; without that attentiveness, the world will relapse into injustice and chaos. My purpose in reviewing these psalms is to point, yet again, to the semantic cluster that reverberates in Israel's liturgic imagination. The key terms are *mispat* and *sedeqah*; we have seen one use of *hesed* and *'emeth* in these psalms (Ps 98:3), and to that we may now add "equity" (*ysr*). That cluster makes clear that the rule of Yhwh is a rule of just, right ordering, and it is that just, right ordering that causes Israel and the peoples to rejoice, and that causes the sea, the fields, and the trees to dance and sing and roar; conditions are now right for an exuberant, generative creation. Because of God's justice, the world can celebrate its status as "very good."

We may, however, notice two things about this liturgic affirmation. First, the cluster of terms—justice, righteousness, and equity—is given no specific content. We may infer specific content of right ordering, but it is not articulated. Second, while we have the active verb "judge," the creator God—who comes in liturgical procession—does not really do anything specific. It is the very act of being there, of coming into the creation, of manifesting awesome sovereignty that brings with it justice. The phrase "lover of justice" means that the creator God is deeply committed to the practice of justice as right ordering; but beyond the generic doxological claim, nothing is specified (Ps 99:4; see Isa 61:8).

This lack of specificity reminds us that we are witnessing the performance of state ritual in the royal temple before the urban elites who govern. We are permitted, in my judgment, to entertain a modicum of reserve about the liturgy, because every regime formulates mantras of justice and *shalom* that become slogans to justify power, but may be very short on policy implementation. Thus, we can gladly recite the pledge, "with liberty and justice for all," but nobody expects that to be taken seriously in any practical way beyond a generic possibility. We may notice that in Psalm 47, one of Mowinckel's psalms, the primary adherents to this God-King are "the people of the God of Abraham." As Westermann has seen, the Abrahamic tradition revolved around blessing—that is, the infusion of the life-force into creation without any of the specifics of deliverance.[5] I do not minimize the importance of this usage, and it is better that we have it than not. But we should not, I think, overappreciate it, as it perhaps reflects common royal claims that function as royal propaganda in the reinforcement of common royal ideology.

We may notice, moreover, that there is here no human agency. Perhaps the genre of these psalms rules out human agency. It is clear that in this collection of enthronement psalms there is no work to be done by human agents. It is all accomplished by the divine sovereign who need only appear in majesty.

To be sure, the royal-temple ideology wants to imagine human agency, to affirm that the human king is a performer of justice. Thus, Psalm 72, a royal psalm, summons the king to justice:

> Give the king your justice, O God,
> and your righteousness to a king's son. (v. 1)

This psalm, moreover, gives specificity that is lacking in the enthronement psalms:

> May he judge your people with righteousness,
> and your poor with justice. . . .
> May he defend the cause of the poor of the people,
> give deliverance to the needy,
> and crush the oppressor. . . .
> For he delivers the needy when they call,
> the poor and those who have no helper.
> He has pity on the weak and the needy, and saves the lives of
> the needy.
> From oppression and violence he redeems their life,
> and precious is their blood in his slight. (vv. 2, 4, 12-14)

Now justice takes on concrete social possibility and social expectation that has in purview the poor, the needy, and the weak, the ones who face and experience oppression and violence. The king and the royal apparatus are presented as ally and advocate for those who suffer in the economy. The prophetic tradition that segues into messianic expectation does the same. Thus in the familiar oracles of Isaiah,

> His authority shall grow continually
> And there shall be endless peace

for the throne of David and his kingdom.
He will establish and uphold it with justice and with
  righteousness
From this time forward and forevermore. (9:7)
He shall not judge by what his eyes see,
or decide by what his ears hear;
but with righteousness he shall judge the poor,
and decide with equity for the meek of the earth;
he shall strike the earth with the rod of his mouth,
and with the breath of his lips he shall kill the wicked.
Righteousness shall be the belt around his waist,
and faithfulness the belt around his loins. (11:3-5)

The first of these oracles anticipates endless *shalom* grounded
in *mispat* and *sedeqah*. The second is more specific in its focus
on the poor and the meek, with a glance at the wicked—that
is, the exploiters who work against the common good of *shalom*
intended by the creator.

Even in Jeremiah, a tradition that has little truck with roy-
alty, we get at least the liturgic clichés about human agency:

> The days are coming, says the Lord, when I will raise up
> for David a righteous Branch, and he shall reign as king and
> deal wisely, and shall execute *justice and righteousness* in the
> land. (23:5)

> In those days and at that time I will cause a righteous
> Branch to spring up for David, and he shall execute *justice
> and righteousness* in the land. (33:15)

And Ezekiel lays out a program for human agency in three
dramatic steps:

(a) The failure of kings to do justice (34:1-6).
(b) The resolve of Yhwh to do kingly justice directly:

> I myself will be the shepherd of my sheep, and I will
> make them lie down, says the Lord. I will seek the
> lost, and I will bring back the strayed, and I will bind
> up the injured, and I will strengthen the weak, but
> the fat and the strong I will destroy. I will feed them
> with justice. (vv. 15-16)

(c) The rule that Yhwh has claimed for God's own self is assigned to the human agent, King David, in time to come:

> I will set up over them one shepherd, my servant David, and he shall feed them; he shall feed them and be their shepherd. (v. 23)

The specificity of the Ezekiel oracle makes one wonder why it is so late before some good bishop could formulate the phrase, "God's preferential option for the poor." The king is to be the great equalizer (speaking of equity!) who functions on behalf of the vulnerable and resourceless in order that they can participate in the luxurious generosity of creation over which the king presides.

It is clear that the royal theology of Jerusalem wants to imagine such a human agent who will do that work. If these several psalms and prophetic oracles are occasioned by the coronations of new kings in Jerusalem as some think, then the reiteration of the slogans is not unlike campaign rhetoric among us that is about "maintaining the middle class" or "care for the less fortunate." Such rhetoric is important, because it at least keeps hope alive. It insists that justice is beyond deconstruction because it is willed and ordained into the very fabric of creation. But justice as viable order is, in this purview, justice *from above*. It is justice that imagines that if the king and the urban elites in Jerusalem are well off, it will all trickle down. I suspect that such royal justice is not unlike the decision to save the banks, because eventually, it is said, homeowners will benefit. But top-down justice seems too often to stop with the banks.

Now the reason I am suspicious of such justice is that there are indications that the royal players in this liturgy were not overly zealous about the matter. They well understood that liturgic mantras are not policy. Let us imagine that Solomon, whose name means *shalom*, is the model performer of royal resolve, for it is said of Solomon, even by the Queen of Sheba:

> Because the Lord loved Israel forever, he has made you king to execute justice and righteousness. (1 Kgs 10:9)

But what follows immediately in that fanciful narrative is this:

> Then she gave the king one hundred twenty talents of gold, a great quantify of spices, and precious stones; never again did spices come in such quantity as that which the queen of Sheba gave to King Solomon. (v. 10)

The narrative goes on to make clear that Solomon's justice and righteousness was transposed into a massive accumulation of commodities, perhaps with a trickle-down anticipation. We may imagine that Psalm 72, the royal psalm, is on the lips of Solomon, for its superscription is "Psalm of Solomon." But Solomon, we know, built a legacy of massive accumulation of spices and clothes and gold and silver, and horses and chariots and proverbs and songs and women, accumulation that surely contradicts "justice and righteousness." By the end of his reign, moreover, we are told that his regime fell apart in a dispute over taxes, because the royal government had taxed the peasants for the sake of indulgence and aggrandizement in the royal cities:

> Your father made our yoke heavy. (1 Kgs 12:4)

And his son, schooled in royal power, had learned nothing:

> My little finger is thicker than my father's loins. Now, whereas my father laid on you a heavy yoke, I will add to your yoke. My father disciplined you with whips, but I will discipline you with scorpions. (vv. 10-11, 14)

And the interpreter, in this text, links this act of taxation to the will of Yhwh for the demise of the dynasty. The Solomon regime is a study in exploitation, though all the while the mantras of the liturgy continued to be performed.

We may venture, moreover, a negative characterization of kingship that the tradition has placed in the mouth of Samuel. The NIV translates, "This is what the king will do." That, however, is too weak, for the wording suggests a normative quality for the king's policies of usurpation. The NRSV is not any better. Both renderings avoid the stunning use of the term *mispat*. Here is the full text in NRSV:

> These will be the ways (*mispat*) of the king who will reign over you: he will take your sons and appoint them to his chariots and to be his horsemen, and to run before his chariots; and he will appoint for himself commanders of thousands and commanders of fifties, and some to plow his ground and to reap his harvest, and to make his implements of war and the equipment of his chariots. He will take your daughters to be perfumers and cooks and bakers. He will take the best of your fields and vineyards and olive orchards and give them to his courtiers. He will take one-tenth of your grain and of your vineyards and give it to his officers and courtiers. He will take your male and female slaves and the best of your cattle and donkeys, and put them to his work. He will take one-tenth of your flocks, and you shall be his slaves. (1 Sam 8:11-17)

The offer is a confiscatory regime that transfers wealth from the common folk to the urban elites who preside over the military economy. But notice this—the governing phrase that we translate, "These will be the ways of the king," in fact renders the term *mispat*: "This will be the king's justice." It is justice viewed from above. It is justice that is committed to control, luxury, and indulgence that is gotten at the expense of the common people who have sons and daughters and fields and olive orchards and vineyards and cattle and donkeys, but who are helpless before the confiscatory capacity of the privileged elite who occupy Jerusalem and manage the big liturgy.

Now you may judge that it is illicit for me to make a connection between the psalms of divine enthronement, the royal psalms and prophetic oracles of anticipation, and the narratives of royal performance. You may want to say, against that connection, that Yhwh is not complicit in such sordid practice. And you may want to suggest that the royal psalms and oracles give voice to the "better angels" of royal power. Perhaps.

I suggest, however, that *justice as order* tends to be *from above*, and so not attentive or attuned to the lesser folk who make the economy work. I make the connection on two counts. First, all of these texts are connected to the Jerusalem establishment or its belated legacy of entitlement and privilege. And second, it all sounds as contemporary as yesterday, in which the maintenance of a viable economic order has enormous costs. These costs, however, are borne for the most part by those with fewest resources. Thus far, justice as order from above permits the repetition of noble sounding mantras that have little real bite. It is an exercise, I submit, in self-deception.

II.

You expect me to say more than that, and of course more than that can be said. There is, in the tradition, a more vigorous, more demanding notion of justice that was not domesticated by the Jerusalem establishment. We may gain access to that more vigorous, more demanding voicing of justice by one more appeal to the enthronement psalms. In Psalm 99, the one that identifies Yhwh as "mighty king, lover of justice," the next verses make an unexpected move from *cosmic imagination* to the specificities of *historical memory*. The move is unexpected, because generic royal liturgies do not often dwell on such concreteness, because such specificity can be disputatious and divisive. But here it is in verses 6-7, a reference that is singular and without parallel in the enthronement psalms:

> Moses and Aaron were among his priests,
> Samuel also was among those who called on his name.
> They cried to the Lord, and he answered them.
> He spoke to them in the pillar of cloud;

they kept his decrees,
and the statutes that he gave them. (99:6-7)

These two verses draw the worship of the elites in Jerusalem back into an older tradition that would have been awkward among them:

- *These verses identify the three great leaders, none of them of royal identity or credential: Moses, Aaron, Samuel, so that the liturgy was called back behind the monarchy.*
- *The verses recall the cry, when they groaned and cried out in their slavery. Jerusalem has become a happy, therapeutic place where never was heard a discouraging word. But now we are required to remember disturbing words and pre-word sounds that shattered the silence of ordered governance. It is like an old-time liturgy designed to tell the tale of old liberation, of old feminist struggle, or old civil rights struggle, and the younger who are well off have no patience for or interest in such struggle. But, insists the tradition, we did cry!*
- *The verses recall that God answered. This is not God without pathos who sits serenely atop the pipe organ. This is a God who is down and dirty among the victims of old, exploitative economy. Such an affirmation that "he answered them" is a cutting reminder against any imagined self-sufficiency.*
- *These verses recall wilderness risk presided over by pillar of cloud, the sort of thing Richard Dawkins would say is magical thinking, but leadership about which the old "magicians" of Pharaoh had not a clue.*
- *These verses ruminate about statutes and ordinances, that is, a people under command, a command unlike the commands of Pharaoh, one that is haunted by Sinai's conditional "if":*

  Now therefore, if you obey my voice and keep my covenant, you shall be my treasured possession out of all the peoples. Indeed, the whole earth is mine, but you shall be for me a priestly kingdom and a holy nation. (Exod 19:5-6)

These two verses in the psalm strike me as an incredible disruption of order from above, and invite thought about justice as *transformation from below*, out of the slave camp to which Yhwh has been summoned.

Now you may think that this is too schematic and that I bet too much on these two singular verses in Psalm 99. But what I want you to consider is that it makes a difference whether justice is

Order from above
or
Transformation from below.

I believe that these two modes of justice are often homogenized or confused, and such confusion or homogenization keeps us from thinking clearly and acting faithfully.

The reference to Moses, Aaron, and the cry requires us to situate our thinking about justice in the world of Pharaoh in the midst of Egypt. Indeed, there is the smell of Egypt about this justice. I say "smell of Egypt" in deliberate reference to the accusation that the slaves made against Moses and Aaron:

> You have brought us into bad odor with Pharaoh and his officials, and have put a sword in their hand to kill us. (Exod 5:21)

You know, slaves never bathe, and they are dirty and smell badly. But the smell of Egypt reverses the odor; it is the smell of injustice that permeates the narrative memory of Israel, not the smell of the slaves.

The beginning of transformative justice is the narrative of injustice performed by Pharaoh. The justice of Sinai voiced in Psalm 99:5-6 makes little sense except with reference to Pharaoh and his narrative of injustice. That narrative of Pharaoh's injustice intended to contain all imaginable social possibility, to control all lines of power, and to dominate all technological capacity. The aim is to so construct governance that nothing is possible or admissible or even imaginable outside of it. As we ponder this narrative of injustice, we may wonder about the historical identity of Pharaoh, if indeed he existed. For sure, we have spent many cubits of ink on that question of historical identification. We will have no doubt, however, that Pharaoh who dominates this narrative of injustice is a recurring type, constantly reappearing wherever absolutizing totalism can gain a foothold.[6]

This narrative is soon told:

1. Pharaoh is a master of abundance. Already in Genesis 12:10-20, when Abraham faced a famine he knew to go to Egypt, that great breadbasket. In that paragraph we see that Pharaoh not only dominated the food supply but had procurement officers to recruit good women for him, including mother Sarah. No doubt, as Wendell Berry asserts, the way women are treated goes with how land (and food) are treated. Pharaoh had ample of land, food, and women.

2. This matter of abundance is beset with anxiety. Pharaoh, we are told, has two nightmares (Gen 41:1-7). And when he finally finds a good Jewish dream interpreter, we learn—concerning seven lean cows devouring seven fat cows and seven good shocks of grain being eaten by seven blighted shocks of grain—that these are dreams about scarcity. In his abundance, Pharaoh had anxiety about running out!

3. When Pharaoh recruits Joseph, the Hebrew, to be his food czar, Pharaoh's program of accumulation is set in motion, given greater impetus by the sign-on of the Hebrew who is now allied with Pharaoh's narrative of injustice. Indeed, for good reason Leon Kass has said that this is the "Egyptianization" of Joseph![7] The one with abundance must have more in order to assuage his anxiety about scarcity. And the only way to accumulate more is to confiscate what belongs to others, especially others who are vulnerable and cannot protect what they have. Pharaoh's totalizing effectiveness, moreover, is so massive and compelling that this son of Israel signs on to manage the confiscatory policy of accumulation. The peasants, we are told, need to secure food from the royal abundance in the face of famine, and Joseph sells them food (Gen 47:14). In the second year of their famine, the peasants need food but have no money for purchase. Not thinking to give them anything free from Pharaoh's massive storehouses, Joseph trades the peasants food for their livestock and so puts them out of business. In the third year of their famine, the peasants again need food, but they have no tradable commodities. As a result, Joseph, acting for Pharaoh, seizes their land and their bodies and reduces them to slavery. But so totalizing is Pharaoh's capacity that the peasants actually express their gratitude to Pharaoh for making them slaves:

> Shall we die before your eyes, both we and our land? Buy us and our land in exchange for food. We with our land will become slaves to Pharaoh; just give us seed, so that we may live and not die, and that the land may not become desolate. . . . You have saved our lives; may it please my lord, we will be slaves to Pharaoh. (Gen 47:19, 25)

4. In the end, Pharaoh's policy of accumulation results in monopoly. He has it all! Except for the property of the exempt priests who benefit from the monopoly:

> So Joseph made it a statute concerning the land of Egypt, and it stands to this day, that Pharaoh should have the fifth. The land of the priests alone did not become Pharaoh's. (v. 26)

5. There the matter is left, until we turn the page to the book of Exodus. Now the very family of Joseph is also reduced to slavery, as the monopoly of the engine of totalism will not stop until it contains all. It does not surprise that the narrative of injustice ends in violence. Why would it not?

> The Egyptians became ruthless in imposing tasks on the Israelites, and made their lives bitter with hard service in mortar and brick and in every kind of field labor. They

were ruthless in all the tasks that they imposed on them.
(Exod 1:13-14)

Because this narrative is not historical reportage but constructed memory, we can see that it is paradigmatic. This sequence is not unfamiliar to us, because it continues to recur before our very eyes. It is a tale of *abundance, anxiety, scarcity, accumulation, monopoly, and eventually violence* in a context where there is no regulatory or restraining force. The narrative provides an angle on injustice from which to consider the urgency of justice. Injustice is the capacity to confiscate what belongs to another in order to satisfy anxiety which, in the process, is free to reduce the losers to helpless victims who are without recourse. This narrative of injustice that preoccupies the Old Testament and Pharaoh is, always and everywhere, the star performer in the narrative.

Thus, in the Psalms the narrative is reperformed:

In the pride of their countenance the wicked say,
"God will not seek it out."
All their thoughts are, "There is no God."

. . .

They sit in ambush in the villages;
in hiding places they murder the innocent.
Their eyes stealthily watch for the helpless;
they lurk in secret like a lion in its covert;
they lurk that they may seize the poor;
they seize the poor and drag them off in their net.
They stoop, they crouch,
and the helpless fall by their might.
They think in their heart, "God has forgotten,
He has hidden his face, he will never see it." (Ps 10:4, 8-11)

Or more familiarly in the prophets:

Hear this, you that trample on the needy,
and bring to ruin the poor of the land,
saying, "When will the new moon be over,
so that we may sell grain,

and the sabbath,
so that we may offer wheat for sale?
We will make the ephah small and the shekel great,
and practice deceit with false balances,
buying the poor for silver
and the needy for a pair of sandals,
and selling the sweepings of the wheat." (Amos 8:4-6)

Alas for those who devise wickedness
and evil deeds on their beds!
When the morning dawns, they perform it,
because it is in their power.
They covet fields and seize them;
houses, and take them away;
they oppress householders and houses,
people and their inheritance. (Mic 2:1-2)

Can I tolerate wicked scales
and a bag of dishonest weights?
Your wealthy are full of violence,
your inhabitants speak lies,
with tongues of deceit in their mouths. (Mic 6:11-12)

Ah, you who make iniquitous decrees,
who write oppressive statutes,
to turn aside the needy from justice
and to rob the poor of my people of their right,
that widows may be your spoil,
and that you may make the orphans your prey! (Isa 10:1-2)

From the least to the greatest of them,
everyone is greedy for unjust gain;
and from prophet to priest,
everyone deals falsely.
They have treated the wound of my people carelessly,
saying "Peace, peace," when there is no peace.
They acted shamefully, they committed abomination;
yet they were not ashamed,
they did not know how to blush. (Jer 6:13-15)

Justice is turned back, and righteousness stands at a distance;
for truth stumbles in the public square,
and uprightness cannot enter.
Truth is lacking,
And whoever turns from evil is despoiled. (Isa 59:14-15)

I propose that the question of justice in Israel's imagination is this: Can that totalizing narrative of injustice be interrupted? Or, put another way: Is there a vantage point from which to imagine life outside the totalizing system of injustice? This is the defining question for Israel; it is, moreover, the recurrently defining question for public life, and now it is an urgent question among us. The gospel, from the outset, is the news that the totalizing system has been, or soon will be interrupted. The Bible is an account of that recurring interruption wrought by divine initiative through human agency. And while that interruption may take many forms, the Exodus narrative identifies for us the characteristic maneuvers essential for interruption—that is, essential to the practice of justice in contexts of systemic injustice. In the wake of the Exodus narrative, the prophets repeatedly create artistic alternatives to the predatory economic policies and practices of the Jerusalem elites. In the Exodus narrative, the interruption includes the following:

1. The initial sly work of the midwives who refuse Pharaoh's dictum to kill the baby boys (Exod 1:15-22). While we do not know Pharaoh's name, we know the names of these courageous women, Shiphrah and Puah. They are celebrated as our first two conscientious objectors who dare imagine that there is life outside the domain of Pharaoh. The interruption of the narrative of injustice requires cunning actions by those who unostentatiously refuse the obedience of injustice. I suppose that these two women embody the work of James C. Scott concerning "hidden transcripts."[8] Their hidden transcript, which they perform at great risk, is the affirmation that "the force" of life is with the slave community.

2. The interruption includes the abrasion of Moses who, in the face of brutalizing forced labor, kills the Egyptian supervisor who was abusing a Hebrew, "one of his kinsmen" (Exod 2:11-21). The interruption of the narrative of injustice requires an abrasion, an escalation from surreptitious cunning defiance to overt abrasion that joins issue with the totalizing. That abrasion makes clear that the hegemony of Pharaoh is not a given but a construct. The violence of Moses of course gives us pause, so that we may not recommend such action. There may be a leap here to violence, but we must observe that every act of emancipation includes a warrant that passes as violence to the totalizers.

3. After the cunning defiance of the women whose names we know and the abrasion of Moses, the interruption becomes more public in the wholesale action of Israel that brings their anguish and suffering to public speech. The anguish and suffering had long been present among the slaves. And Pharaoh did not worry about that. What matters is public speech. The work of justice brings pain to speech in a way that will be noticed:

> After a long time the king of Egypt died. The Israelites groaned under their slavery and cried out. (Exod 2:23)

The cry is not addressed to anyone. It is simply the bodily protest against abusive violence that is the most elemental insistence on justice, and so an exposé of injustice.

4. That cry sets the juices of emancipation in motion, because it is the cry that evokes the first interest of the emancipatory God in the plight of those who suffer injustice. It is in response to the daring, insistent voice of pain that Yhwh responds:

> Out of slavery their cry for help rose up to God. God heard their groaning, and God remembered his covenant with Abraham, Isaac, and Jacob. God looked upon the Israelites and God took notice of them. (vv. 23-25)

The God who has now noticed and would not have noticed except for the cry now appears in a burning bush and identifies God's own self as the promissory God of the Genesis narrative. That self-presentation permits Yhwh now to stake out a claim to emancipation, to authorize life outside the claims of Pharaoh. Yhwh gives voice to a resolved divine agency:

> I have observed the misery of my people who are in Egypt; I have heard their cry on account of their taskmasters. Indeed, I know their suffering, and I have come down to deliver them from the Egyptians, and bring them up out of that land to a good and broad land, a land flowing with milk and honey. . . . The cry of the Israelites has now come to me; I have seen how the Egyptians oppress them. (3:7-9)

The text has no doubt that Yhwh has freedom beyond Pharaoh's totality and now authorizes the Israelites to depart that constructed world of injustice to an alternative life amid the justice of Yhwh's domain.

5. Given the big resolve of Yhwh, however, we are surprised that after the self-presentation of Yhwh, in verse 10 Yhwh assigns Moses as human agent:

> So come, I will send you to Pharaoh to bring my people, the Israelites, out of Egypt.

Finally, justice as socioeconomic political recovery from the debilitating injustice of totalism requires human agency. To be sure, it is God-designated human agency, but unmistakably human agency.

This narrative constitutes a drama of departure, the refusal of and departure from the ideology of injustice, in order to enter an alternative life. The road to alternative, in the Exodus narrative, is not an easy one, because the totalism does not readily cede legitimacy to alternative. The extended plague narrative is a contest, a testing of wills and a testing of capacity, to see if the will for justice can outlast the intransigence of injustice. It is, as you know, a close run. But by the end of the confrontation, even Pharaoh, the master of injustice, acknowledges that the truth of the future lies beyond his mechanism of accumulation, monopoly, and violence:

> Rise up, go away from my people, both you and the Israelites! Go, worship the Lord, as you said. Take your flocks and your herds, as you have said, and be gone. And bring a blessing on me too! (12:31-32)

It is no wonder that Miriam and the other women dance and sing of freedom from the killing force of injustice. Justice is no theoretical notion. It is as practical and immediate as bodily pain and bodily possibility:

> Sing to the Lord, for he has triumphed gloriously;
> horse and rider he has thrown into the sea. (15:21)

It is no accident that Miriam comments on "horse and rider," the tools of military control and imperial intimidation. It is finally the coercive control imposed by the rule of Pharaoh that is defied. The horse is the emblem of such massive and intimidating power, the aura of which is now decisively broken. The story of Israel, the counterstory to Pharaoh, concerns Israel's departure from Pharaoh's land of administered scarcity to the zone of inexplicable generosity. It is remarkable that they left Egypt. It is equally remarkable that two verses into the wilderness they want to go back to the security of enslavement:

> The whole congregation of the Israelites complained against Moses and Aaron in the wilderness. The Israelites said to them, "If only we had died by the hand of the Lord in the land of Egypt, when we sat by the fleshpots and ate our fill of bread; for you have brought us out into the wilderness to kill this whole assembly with hunger." (16:2-3)

Such a grip does Pharaoh have on the imagination of Israel that wilderness seems to them a zone of death. "Wilderness" is a place, in Israelite imagination, where there are no adequate, viable life-support systems. It is remarkable that as they can finally turn their attention away from Pharaoh to notice the wilderness, the wilderness, the place without viable life supports, turns out to be occupied territory.

They look to the wilderness, and the glory of the Lord appears in a cloud (16:10). Who knew? It is remarkable, in the face of contention and quarreling, that wilderness is now seen to be God-occupied. Pharaoh had long insisted that there was nothing viable outside his sphere. But the wilderness turns out to be a place of abundance. It dazzles, after Pharaoh's totalism, to discover that outside of that totalism, another life is possible.

- It is a place for meat:

  In the evening quails came up and covered the camp. (16:13)

- It is a place of bread:

  In the morning there was a layer of dew around the camp. When the layer of dew lifted, there on the surface of the wilderness was a fine flaky substance, as fine as frost on the ground. When the Israelites saw it, they said to one another, "What is it?" For they did not know what it was. Moses said to them, "It is bread that the Lord has given you to eat." (16:13-15)

- It is a place for water:

  "Strike the rock, and water will come out of it, so that the people may drink." Moses did so, in the sight of the elders of Israel. (17:6)

Meat, bread, water—who knew? Pharaoh had long insisted that there is nothing viable outside his sphere. Who knew that there would be meat he had not butchered, bread he had not baked, water he had not taken from the Nile? The hard journey to justice is the departure from the world of confiscating parsimony in order to enter the world of surging, inexplicable abundance. That world permits justice. So it is with the bread of abundance:

This is what the Lord has commanded: "Gather as much of it as each of you needs, an omer to a person according to the number of persons, all providing for those in their own tents." The Israelites did so, some gathering more, some less. But when they measured it with an omer, those who gathered much had nothing over, and those who gathered little had no shortage; they gathered as much as each of them needed. (16:16-18)

There is, however, also written a warning against accumulation, for accumulation will eventuate in Pharaoh and transpose the bread of abundance into the bread of parsimony and soon into bondage. And the reason is that some will have too much and they will think they are the bakers. It is written, moreover, that the bread of abundance is especially provided in a double portion for the seventh day of sabbath. What a staggering measure of confidence and assurance! Even in the precariousness of wilderness, sabbath rest is specified, that day when Israel acknowledges that its life is a gift and not a possession. So far as we know, no one got a day off in Egypt, not Pharaoh or his slaves, because the force of accumulation is insatiable. It occurred to me to juxtapose this provision in Exodus with the indictment of Amos:

Eat it today, for today is a sabbath to the Lord; today you will not find it in the field. Six days you shall gather it; but on the seventh day, which is a sabbath, there will be none.

(Exod 16:26)

When will the new moon be over
so that we may sell grain;
and the sabbath, so that we may offer wheat for sale?

(Amos 8:5)

Sabbath is the disciplined refusal of the insatiable demands of injustice that prey upon the neighbor and that permit the illusion of self-sufficiency.

III.

I call attention now to the decisive interpretive move I have made thus far. I began with the liturgy of Zion that makes all the right sounds of justice, righteousness, and equity. But I suggested that that liturgy is in the environs of, and I dare say in the interest of, the urban elite in Jerusalem. In that liturgy there is no specificity about justice, and there is no human agency. It is, I suggest, a great seduction to voice those mantras in such a context. But I find an opening for more than that in Psalm 99:6-7, the last of the enthronement psalms, to push back from Zion's liturgy to the more elemental (I do not say earlier) memory of Moses, Aaron, Sinai, and Exodus. There is, I think, some irony in the inclusion of these Sinai verses in the Zion liturgy, as though Zion intended to possess the Sinai memory and to subordinate it to the grand claims of Zion. I suggest, however, that these verses offer something of a deconstructive move. Because some alert child who notices the shift from

> Worship [the Lord] at his footstool [meaning the temple] (v. 5)

to

> They cried to the Lord (v. 6)

will ask in time to come, "What mean these verses?"
And then you shall tell them:

> "It is because of what the Lord did for me when I came out of Egypt." It shall serve for you as a sign on your hand and as a reminder on your forehead, so that the teaching of the Lord may be on your lips; for with a strong hand the Lord brought you out of Egypt. (Exod 13:8-9)

And right there, in the Zion liturgy, in whispered conviction, the grand reassuring cadences of Zion are devolved into the narrative of interruption that goes beneath temple mantras to the tale of emancipation, abundance, and eventually justice in which the neighbors share life-goods.

But when they measured it with an omer, those who gathered much had nothing over, and those who gathered little
had no shortage; they gathered as much as each of them
needed. (16:18)

No shortage . . . because of no accumulation!

This is and always is a contemporary contest. It is a contest between Pharaonic anxiety expressed in the nightmarish
sequence of *scarcity, accumulation, monopoly, and violence*, juxta-
posed to *emancipatory abundance*. In our own time, I judge that
the role of totalism is played in our society by corporate capitalism, propelled by market ideology, inured to individualism,
sustained by a strong military, and legitimated by the entitle-
ments of patriotic exceptionalism . . . a mouthful indeed! That
ideology is indeed totalizing; it claims that there is and can
be no alternative. With only a little imagination, we can see
Pharaonic impulses being reperformed, because the ones with
the most are the ones who worry about running out for lack
of bricks, and that in turn propels accumulation, wherein a
few have nearly acquired a monopoly, with violence against
all the others carefully disguised. This is perhaps a good-faith
enterprise, as was Pharaoh's—the practitioners really believe
it. Or perhaps a not good-faith enterprise, but the mantras of
"freedom and faith" are knowing covers that function to hide
the work of government as the transfer of wealth. Whether
good faith or simply convenient cover, this is the old, old story
of injustice become the new, new song of self-sufficiency func-
tioning in a way that denies and defeats the common good.

In contemporary performance of that enterprise, the
counterrole is played, as it was then, by a "mixed multitude"
(Exod 12:38) or, better, an "undisciplined rabble" without credential or identity.[9] It was and is an uneven drama of legitimated power in contest with ragtag hopers whose hope is
rooted in cries of pain and suffering that confiscatory injustice evokes. That "mixed multitude" consists in all those who
refuse, deny, or doubt the totalizing claims, and who continue

to keep imagining and attempting alternative modes of life, and who keep experimenting with the strange virtues of justice that take various forms of neighborliness. In Pharaoh's Egypt there were no neighbors or neighborhoods. There was only the corporate structure, and all the others were dispensable forms of cheap labor, threat, or at best inconvenience. So the issue is joined.

I suggest that the Bible is the master script for that contest that is always being reperformed. There are ample voices in Scripture that want to defend and protect the monopoly via the rigors of punishment and the disciplines of purity. But the main flow of the script is to insist that such anti-neighborliness is unsustainable; and so we get prophetic voices and sapiential voices and psalmic voices who tell otherwise.

Derivative from the biblical script, I could think of two renderings of this contest that merit attention. First, in his puckish answer to Richard Dawkins and Christopher Hitchens, the two whom together he terms "Ditchens," Terry Eagleton makes the case for biblical faith claims of reality outside the reductionism of Enlightenment reason, with validation of what he terms "the scum of the earth."[10] The ground of validity, he proposes, is that the script and the God who occupies the script attend to the scum, all the losers like widows, orphans, and immigrants, and publicans and sinners, all the disqualified who are not able to make enough bricks to advance in Pharaoh's domain:

> Jesus, unlike most responsible American citizens appears to do no work, and is accused of being a glutton and a drunkard. He is presented as homeless, propertyless, celibate, peripatetic, socially marginal, disdainful of kinsfolk, without a trade, a friend of outcasts and pariahs, averse to material possessions, without fear for his own safety, careless abut purity regulations, critical of traditional authority, a thorn in the side of the Establishment, and a scourge of the rich and powerful.[11] . . . The morality Jesus preaches is reckless, extravagant, improvident, over-the-top, a scandal to

actuaries and a stumbling block to real estate agents: forgive your enemies, give away your cloak as well as your coat, turn the other cheek, love those who insult you, walk the extra mile, take no thought for tomorrow.[12] . . . To the outrage of Zealots, Pharisees, and right-wing rednecks of all ages, this body is dedicated in particular to all those losers, deadbeats, riffraff, and colonial collaborators who are not righteous but flamboyantly unrighteous—who either live in chronic transgression of the Mosaic law or, like the Gentiles, fall outside of its sway altogether.[13] . . . The only authentic image of this violently loving God is a tortured and executed political criminal, who dies in an act of solidarity with what the Bible calls the *anawim*, meaning the destitute and dispossessed. Crucifixion was reserved by the Romans for political offenses alone. The *anawim*, in Pauline phrase, are the shit of the earth—the scum and refuse of society who constitute the cornerstone of the new form of human life known as the kingdom of God. Jesus himself is consistently presented as their representative.[14]

This exposition of Eagleton draws out the extreme implications of the Exodus contest for justice, a contest that runs through the life of Jesus and the life of the church.

Second, Enrique Dussel, one of our great voices of liberation ethics, has described in a very dense book the power of totalism.[15] He identifies the cry through which there is an opening beyond that totalism for the flourishing of the genuinely human. He quotes Gramsci that the praxis of liberation is "the small door through which the Messiah might enter."[16] He avers:

The victim who becomes conscious, who erupts with a revolutionary praxis, produces a rupture of "continuous time." He or she erupts remembering . . . other liberatory-messianic moments of past history.[17]

Alluding to Horkheimer and Adorno, he judges that the dialogue

is also a cry, a protest, and an exercise of critical-ethical reason at the philosophical level.[18]

And then Dussel goes on to connect that cry that is acceptable

> to the ears of a Nicaraguan, of the black African of South
> Africa, of the Palestinian in the Israelite-occupied territory,
> or of the homeless in New Delhi . . . or New York.[19]

It is this cry that funds historical possibility. Thus:

> After a long time the king of Egypt died. The Israelites
> groaned under their slavery and cried out. Out of the slav-
> ery their cry for help rose up to God. (Exod 2:23-24)

And in a famous wordplay in Isaiah 5:7, with our favorite word pair:

> He expected justice (*mispat*), but saw bloodshed (*mispah*);
> righteousness (*sedeqah*), but heard a cry (*za'aqah*)!

The wordplay cannot be recognized in English; but the contrast is between *justice and cry*, the central abrasion of the Exodus narrative and of all human history in the presence of this emancipatory God. (See the juxtaposition of "justice and cry" in the parable of Luke 18:1-7.) That cry echoes, all the way down to Bartimaeus:

> Many sternly ordered him to be quiet, but he cried even
> more loudly, "Son of David, have mercy on me!" (Mark 10:48)

Justice is voicing the cry, hearing the cry, and reorganizing social power in response to the cry.

IV.

Finally, I have wondered if, after we have observed Sinai, we can return to the liturgies of Zion.[20] I had the following thoughts about the ways in which the cry of Sinai may be honored in the liturgies of Zion.

1. In 1 Kings 8, we have the grand pageant of the dedication of Solomon's temple. The ark figures prominently, understood as the old totem on which sat the invisible God. Sinai is being transferred to Zion. That move, moreover, evokes a great choral anthem in which God promises to dwell in Jerusalem forever (8:12-13). Yhwh has become a permanent resident in the claims of the Jerusalem elite . . . game, set, match!

Except that the biblical text will not let the totalism rest easy. In verse 9, right there in the middle of the pageant, someone, likely the custodian, looked into the ark:

> There was nothing in the ark except the two tablets of stone that Moses had placed there at Horeb, when the Lord made a covenant with the Israelites, when they came out of the land of Egypt.

There was no God there, because God is not domesticated. There were only "the two tablets of stone"—that is, the commandments of Sinai. This counterverse 9 insists that the real worship concerns the Sinai stuff, and not the ease of the pageant of Zion. That counterverse is reinforced, moreover, by the exclamation of verse 27 in the mouth of Solomon just after the procession and anthem:

> But will God indeed dwell on the earth? Even the heaven and the highest heaven cannot contain you, much less this house that I have built!

The totalism of Zion—dynasty and temple—cannot contain the great creator God who is on the loose in emancipatory ways. The mantras of injustice sustained by legitimating liturgy are a hoax!

2. Consequently we may ask, Can Sinai be performed in Zion? In the Old Testament, we have only one clear attestation of that possibility. It is evident that the Deuteronomists have portrayed Josiah, the good king, as a loyal practitioner of the Sinai tradition. And Jeremiah, child of the Deuteronomists, can say of Josiah, father of Jehoiakim:

> Did not your father eat and drink
> and do *justice and righteousness?*
> Then it was well with him.
> He judged the cause of the poor and needy;
> then it was well. (Jer 22:15-16)

This is a breathtaking declaration. It asserts that Josiah was allied with the cause of the poor and the needy (as in Solomon's Psalm 72!), that he lived to do *mispat* and *sedeqah*, and that therefore he prospered. He is a carrier and a performer of the Sinai commands. And then Jeremiah adds, in the poem,

Is not this to know me? (v. 16)

Knowing Yhwh—amid the pretensions of Jehoiakim—is solidarity with the vulnerable. Knowing Yhwh is the practice of neighborly justice.

The poem contrasts this father with the son, a king who did not get it:

Woe to him who builds his house by *unrighteousness*,
and his upper rooms by *injustice*;
who makes his neighbors work for nothing,
and does not give them their wages;
who says "I will build myself a spacious house
with large upper rooms,"
and who cuts out windows for it,
paneling with cedar
and painting it with vermillion. (vv. 13-14)

King Jehoiakim, not unlike Solomon, specialized in self-indulgent extravagance. Of necessity, he relied on cheap labor. Injustice, inattentiveness to the poor and needy, will almost always include the litmus test of cheap labor on which the unjust flourishing of the masters of totalism depends. We get the simple equation:

Father Josiah: king after the manner of Sinai, whose regime prospered;
Son Jehoiakim: king in the obdurate ways of Zion, whose regime was unsustainable.

3. The Josiah connection, the clearest interface of the Sinai tradition with the orbit of injustice, calls to mind the single commandment concerning royal power—that is, the only regulation of the economic, political power of the elite.

That commandment, with its retrospective eye on Solomon the accumulator, prohibits royal accumulation:

> He must not acquire many horses for himself . . . and he must not acquire many wives for himself, or else his heart will turn away; also silver and gold he must not acquire in great quantity for himself. (Deut 17:16-17)

Horses, wives, silver, gold . . . all of which sounds a lot like hoarding wealth and power. That is prohibited. And then the counter, in this same paragraph, is this:

> When he has taken the throne of his kingdom, he shall have a copy of this law written for him in the presence of the levitical priests. It shall remain with him and he shall read in it all the days of his life, so that he may learn to fear the Lord his God, diligently observing all the words of this law and these statutes, neither exalting himself above other members of the community nor turning aside from the commandment, either to the right or to the left. (vv. 18-20)

Instead of economic accumulation, spend time pondering the rules of neighborliness written in the Torah. Attention to these rules of neighborliness will keep one mindful of the powerful self as neighbor who will not exalt self over other members of the community. And, says Moses at the end of the commandment, that is the way for a long, good life with order and stability, an alternative to a short unhappy life of accumulation.

4. Finally, I mention two texts that bespeak what a practitioner of justice looks like. In Psalm 112:

> Wealth and riches are in their houses,
> and their righteousness endures forever.
> They rise in the darkness as a light for the upright;
> they are gracious, merciful, and righteous.
> It is well with those who deal generously and lend,
> who conduct their affairs with justice.
> For the righteous will never be moved;
> they will be remembered forever.
> They are not afraid of evil tidings;

their hearts are firm, secure in the Lord.
Their hearts are steady, they will not be afraid;
in the end they will look in triumph on their foes. (vv. 3-8)

The righteous person is not the one who has holy scruples, but whose life is well situated in the neighborhood. Such a man has durable righteousness, delighting in the commandments. Such a woman is gracious, merciful, righteous. Such a person conducts affairs with justice. Such a one is generous, lends, is never destabilized, steady, unafraid. The wicked, who are none of these, gnash their teeth in envy:

The wicked see it and are angry;
they gnash their teeth and melt away;
the desire of the wicked comes to nothing. (v. 10)

Job, in his self-defense, marks his own practice of justice:

If I have rejected the cause of my male or female slaves,
when they brought a complaint against me . . .
If I have withheld anything that the poor desired,
or have caused the eyes of the widow to fail,
or have eaten my morsel alone,
and the orphan has not eaten from it—
for from my youth I reared the orphan like a father,
and from my mother's womb I guided the widow—
if I have seen anyone perish for lack of clothing,
or a poor person without covering, whose loins have not
    blessed me,
and who was not warmed with the fleece of my sheep;
if I have raised my hand against the orphan,
because I saw I had supporters at the gate . . .
If I have made gold my trust,
or called fine gold my confidence;
if I have rejoiced because my wealth was great,
or because my hand had gotten much . . . (31:13, 16-21, 24-25)[21]

Both the psalmist and Job are models of the Sinai enterprise. It worked well for the psalmist who prospered. It did not work so well for Job who suffered. But whether it works or not, they persisted. Both of these witnesses insist that the claims of righteousness and justice are rooted in the narrative, rooted in the commandments, rooted beneath that in God's own intention. The text invites participation in this struggle to create and perform a life not seduced by a totalism that offers the illusion of life alone against the neighbor. These witnesses would agree with Derrida. Justice is not deconstructible. Whereas totalism is committed to the status quo and is always being deconstructed by the Spirit, the claims of justice situate us in the trajectory of the possible beyond all present arrangements.

3

GRACE
The Inexplicable Reach Beyond

Morton Smith, a Jewish scholar, wrote an article in 1952 on the "common theology" of the ancient Near East.[1] After him, Norman Gottwald probed "common theology" more deeply and more expansively.[2] By the phrase "common theology," Smith and Gottwald refer to the pattern of theological themes that recur all over the Near East for a very long time. Smith identified six themes in that common theology:

1. One high God above all others in a world of many gods.
2. The effectiveness of this high God in all spheres of life . . . history, nature, and morality, both legal and civic.
3. The high God is represented by symbols of power: sun, bull, father, king, with an accent on masculine symbolization.
4. This high God punishes offenders against his will and rewards those compliant with his will; thus, God is just toward offenders, merciful toward the compliant.
5. The relations of this high God to the worshiping people are "essentially contractual." There is a direct

relation between obedience and disobedience to God and the fortunes of the people.

6. There are prophets who announce appropriate punishments and rewards.

It is clear that this theology functions as a guarantee for social order that readily slips over into social control. There is no doubt, moreover, that this theology serves as a model for the organization of sociopolitical order and provides a warrant and legitimacy for high-ordering human governance.

By the use of the term "common," Smith and Gottwald intend to suggest that this theology was present as well in ancient Israel and thus in the Old Testament. Indeed, it is now argued by Erhard Gerstenberger, following Rainer Albertz, that this theology served the state in ancient Israel, and that beneath the radar of official religion there was a "lesser religion" of family, clan, and village that allowed for much more intimacy, friendliness, and gentleness in relationship to God.[3] But the big picture offers what I have termed "structure legitimation" that functioned to legitimate social order, social control, and human governance beyond challenge.[4]

This common theology has three obvious manifestations in the Old Testament and constitutes a pattern of faith to which appeal is often made when one wants to speak pejoratively about "the Old Testament."

1. The normative articulation of common theology in the Old Testament is the book of Deuteronomy, offered as an exposition of the covenant of Sinai. The book of Deuteronomy is structured around an extended set of commandments that some suggest is ordered according to the Ten Commandments of Mount Sinai. That legal corpus is followed by a brief recital of blessings and curses in Deuteronomy 27. There is a reference to blessings that are not stated (Deut 27:12); in fact, only curses are actually voiced in the text (vv. 15-26). This recital, moreover, is followed by a more extended voicing of sanctions in chapter 28. We are offered only four blessings (vv. 3-6), plus a hortatory exposition that is dominated by the conditionality of obedience:

> If you keep the commandments of the Lord your God and walk in his ways. (v. 9)

> If you obey the commandments of the Lord your God, which I am commanding you today, by diligently doing them. (v. 13)

> If you do not turn aside from any of the words I am commanding you today, either to the right or to the left, following other gods to serve them. (v. 14)

The long chapter, however, is dominated by a recital of curses, first a catalogue of four curses that correspond to the four blessings (vv. 16-19), and then a development of curses that goes on until verse 68—sum, fifty-three verses. The core teaching of Deuteronomy is summarized in Deuteronomy 30:15-20:

> See, I have set before you today life and prosperity, death and adversity. *If* you obey the commandments of the Lord your God that I am commanding you today, by loving the Lord your God, walking in his ways, and observing his commandments, decrees, and ordinances, *then* you shall live and become numerous, and the Lord your God will bless you in the land that you are entering to possess. But *if* your heart turns away and you do not hear, but are led astray to bow down to other gods and serve them, I declare to you today that you shall perish; you shall not live long in the land that you are crossing the Jordan to enter and possess. I call heaven and earth to witness against you today that I set before you life and death, blessings and curses. Choose life so that you and your descendants may live, loving the Lord your God, obeying him, and holding fast to him; for that mean life to you and length of days, so that you may live in the land that the Lord swore to give to your ancestors, to Abraham, to Isaac, and to Jacob.

The whole is governed by the two "ifs" of condition matched by two "thens" (one implied in v. 18), the "if-then" of "common theology." That same rhetorical pattern is made clear, moreover, in 1 Kings 9:4-7, where the "if-then" symmetry is complete. And again the negative warning receives vigorous elaboration in verses 8-9. The Deuteronomist, with his *quid pro quo* calculus, is insistent in affirming that conduct matters; by policy and by behavior, we choose our futures. This affirmation is relentless and uncompromising.

2. A second exposition of common theology is offered in the prophetic speeches of judgment that are presented as lawsuits.[5] In a variety of configurations, these prophetic speeches of judgment consist in "indictment" for violations of covenantal commandments that are an affront to the God of the covenant, and "sentences" that articulate the penalties that come in the wake of such disobedience:

> Hear the word of the Lord,
> O people of Israel;
> for the Lord has an indictment against the inhabitants
>   of the land.
> There is no faithfulness or loyalty,
> and no knowledge of God in the land.
> Swearing, lying, and murder,
> and stealing and adultery break out;
> bloodshed follows bloodshed.
> *Therefore* the land mourns,
> and all who live in it languish;
> together with the wild animals
> and the birds of the air,
> even the fish of the sea are perishing. (Hos 4:1-3)

> Hear this, you rulers of the house of Jacob
> and chiefs of the house of Israel,
> who abhor justice and pervert all equity,
> who build Zion with blood
> and Jerusalem with wrong!
> Its rulers give judgment for a bribe,
> its priests teach for a price,

its prophets give oracles for money;
Yet they lean on the Lord and say,
"Surely the Lord is with us!
No harm shall come upon us."
Therefore because of you
Zion shall be plowed as a field;
Jerusalem shall become a heap of ruins,
and the mountain of the house a wooded height. (Mic 3:9-12)

Where have you not been lain with?
By the waysides you have sat waiting for lovers, like a nomad in
    the wilderness.
You have polluted the land
with your whoring and wickedness.
Therefore the showers have been withheld,
and the spring rain has not come. (Jer 3:2-3)

The linkage between disobedience and sanction, between indictment and sentence, is accomplished very often by a "therefore" that connects matters in prophetic poetry that might not be otherwise linked. This poetry can proceed as it does because it assumes a tight covenantal connection between disobedience and punishment, a linkage guaranteed by the oversight of the high God, Yhwh.

3. A third articulation of this common theology is found in the sapiential teaching of the book of Proverbs. It is likely that many of these sayings have their locus in clan or family, so that we may see the function of common theology in social locations of less power and prestige; for even in village life a careful observer could see that certain behaviors result in certain outcomes, for good or for ill. Thus:

A slack hand causes poverty,
but the hand of the diligent makes rich.
A child who gathers in summer is prudent,
but a child who sleeps in harvest brings shame. (10:4-5)

Hatred stirs up strife, but love covers all offenses. (v. 12)

The righteous will never be removed,
but the wicked will not remain in the land. (v. 30)

To guarantee loans for a stranger brings trouble,
but there is safety in refusing to do so. (11:15)

Some give freely, yet grow all the richer;
others withhold what is due, and only suffer want. (v. 24)

The examples are endless; the wording is terse, without elaboration. Gerhard von Rad, however, has shown that these proverbs are not glib surface observations, but reflect a deep sense of the dynamism and coherence of the created order.[6] The accumulation of evidence is enough that Klaus Koch has seen that the teaching of the book of Proverbs attests to an instruction in "deeds-consequences," wherein certain deeds reliably yield certain outcomes.[7] It occurs to me that much scientific investigation is a parallel attempt to determine what the outcomes of deeds are, whether "smoking kills" or "exercise produces health," and if so, how much exercise or how many carbs or how much protein, etc.? Patrick Miller, in the wake of the work of Koch, has shown with examples from Jeremiah that the pronouncement of judgment in the prophets often makes the punishment to be quite like the affront of which Israel is accused, so that the offense committed comes back upon the perpetrator in kind.[8]

And if Miller can identify a connection from sapiential teaching to prophetic anticipation, Erhard Gerstenberger has proposed that the simple direct prohibition of the Sinai Torah, "Thou shalt not," may have its origin in the simple familial prohibition, "Thou shalt not touch a hot stove, thou shalt not run out into the street," because the outcomes are easy to anticipate in an ordered world where actions produce consequences.[9] Thus, we may see that there is a rich convergence in these three articulations of faith—covenantal, prophetic, sapiential—without determining priority or direction of influence. We may notice, moreover, that in the great lyrical poem of Job, both Job and his friends agree about common theology. The friends work backward from Job's suffering to Job's unidentified but certain offense. And Job does not dissent from this assumption, but only wants evidence of an offense that could justify the sanction of suffering.

Now when this common theology—variously voiced in covenantal, prophetic, and sapiential cadences—was used as a script for Israel's royal history, it was easy enough, and surely inevitable, to see that the anticipated sanctions of the prophets had come to fruition in the destruction of Jerusalem, its king, and its temple because of the working of common theology. Such a reading made it easy enough to see that Babylon was simply an instrument of Yhwh; it is Yhwh who implemented covenant curses, who had guaranteed the consequences of a long history of unacceptable policies and deeds, who had brought an end to a failed relationship. This is indeed "the end" anticipated by Amos (8:2). Israel is now Jeremiah's broken pot that "cannot be mended" (Jer 19:10-11). The story comes to an end, brought about by Israel's long history of defiant disobedience. It is thus no wonder that the grief songs of Lamentations should end enigmatically in Lamentations 5:22:

> . . . unless you have utterly rejected us,
> and are angry with us beyond measure.

It is not clear if the statement at the end of Lamentations is a question or an indicative; either way the poet articulates "utterly rejected" and "angry beyond measure." And we have the equally enigmatic final word of Job in 42:6 that may be, depending on one's reading, an act of consent and yielding, or defiance. In both cases, the unthinkable is thought and the unspeakable is spoken, albeit with less than clarity. The story has become unsustainable, because the high God will not be mocked.

I add only this: common theology is alive, well, and pervasive among us. It is a sanction against those who do not shape up and perform. It is theology that serves as a confirmation for those who live blessed lives of prosperity because they have kept "Torah." It is a tool of reprimand and punishment for those who do not measure up and are left behind—we dare say, willfully left behind—and so it propels the "war on the poor." In a lighter but no less serious way, the same common theology of social control is evident in our consumer-oriented Christmas festival of self-indulgence:

> He knows if you've been naughty or nice;
> He knows if you've been bad or good,
> so be good for goodness sake!

We manage, in our anxiety, to infuse a bit of common theology into this most self-giving of all Christian celebrations. And then it ends with coal to bad children, with excommunication for the lingering poor in the economy. Such a perspective serves to confirm the reliability of Yhwh's rule and, at the same time, confirms the virtue of those who prosper. In the end, however, Israel's story is longer than that!

II.

After 587 BCE, when the "structure legitimating" work of common theology had been exhausted, Israel had no ground on which to anticipate a future, for the divine promise to David (2 Sam 7:14-16; see Ps 89:39-51) and to Solomon (1 Kgs 8:12-13) had failed. It is, however, a remarkable move in the Old Testament that that context of exhausted possibility in exile turned out to be an inexplicable but unmistakable venue for new possibility. Jeremiah puts it most succinctly:

> The people who survived the sword
> found grace in the wilderness.
> When Israel sought for rest,
> the Lord appeared to him from far away.
> I have loved you with an everlasting love;
> therefore I have continued my faithfulness to you. (31:2-3)

The wilderness, here a symbol for the displacement of exile, is a place from which nothing is expected, because it lacks all the visible supports for a viable life. These astonishing assurances extend beyond the reach of ordinary possibility and beyond the reach of the ordinary high God of common theology. Indeed, we will rightly expect the high God to be eagerly distant from such a context. To the contrary, however, the wilderness of exile turned out to be a generative venue for this high God. Israel expected drought and desolation, perhaps scorpions. But instead Israel found grace! This God appeared to Israel "from far away." And the reason for this inexplicable appearance of God in the wilderness is an everlasting love of continuing fidelity (*hesed*). It turns out that Yhwh's covenant with Israel was not limited to quid pro quo assumptions of covenantal, prophetic, and sapiential symmetry. Yhwh pushed outside and beyond such symmetry, and so generated possibility that could never be available in common theology. Now the divine commitment to Israel is not governed by the conditional "if" of Sinai. Now the gift of the future is not measured by obedience. So Jeremiah can continue his lyric of possibility:

> Again I will build you, and you shall be built,
> O virgin Israel!
> Again you shall take your tambourines,
> and go forth in the dance of the merrymakers.
> Again you shall plant vineyards on the mountains of Samaria;
> the planters shall plant,
> and enjoy the fruit. (vv. 4-5)

The threefold "again" of building, dancing, and planting is reperformance of old divine generosity for which there is now no ground. And so the narrative of fidelity continues, not dependent on Israel's responding fidelity, but now based on a divine fidelity marked by generosity that refuses common theology. The push of the divine reach boggles the mind, as it must have boggled the minds of those displaced people.

Israel muffed its first chance with Yhwh. And now, beyond explanation or expectation, it is offered a second chance. This second chance is very different; it is given in an awareness of Yhwh's new *receptiveness* to Israel's return to obedience and fidelity. Return (repentance) to faithful obedience now becomes the watchword of the second chance. Israel has to decide for obedience. But divine grace is the allowance that Israel may decide, its old, long-term failure notwithstanding.

1. Hans Walter Wolff has discerned that the old quid pro quo calculus of Deuteronomy 5–28 is now bracketed by two texts that push outside the symmetry of covenantal sanctions.[10] Thus, in Deuteronomy 4, after a warning that Yhwh is "a devouring fire" (v. 24), Israel is pushed to repentance, after idolatry and corruption that lead to scattering; so Moses asserts:

> From there [that is, from exile, from wilderness] you will seek the Lord your God, and you will find him if you search after him with all your heart and soul. In your distress, when all these things have happened to you in time to come, you will return to the Lord your God and heed him. (vv. 29-30)

The return is to hearing and heeding—that is, covenantal obedience. And the ground for such a project is this:

> Because the Lord your God is a merciful God, he will neither abandon you nor destroy you; he will not forget the covenant with your ancestors that he swore to them. (v. 31)

Not abandoned, as in common theology! Not destroyed, not forgotten! Because this is a "merciful" God who keeps promises that lie outside the symmetry.

That declaration is matched in Deuteronomy 30 by a longer echo of the same assurance:

> . . . if you call them to mind among all the nations where the Lord your God has driven you, and return to the Lord your God, and you and your children obey with all your heart and with all your soul, just as I am commanding you today, then the Lord your God will restore your fortunes and have

> compassion on you, gathering you again from all the peoples
> among whom the Lord your God has scattered you. (vv. 1-3)

A return to obedience evokes the compassion of the gathering
God who will end exile:

> For the Lord will again take delight in prospering you, just
> as he delighted in prospering your ancestors, when you obey
> the Lord your God by observing his commandments and
> decrees that are written in this book of the law, because you
> turn to the Lord your God with all your heart and with all
> your soul. (vv. 9-10)

The future is all about a turn to obedience to the scroll of
the Torah, in this case, the commands of Deuteronomy. The
rhetoric is formulaic; we should not miss, however, the abrupt
radicality of the divine offer. Restoration requires obedience. The curse no longer pertains, because the exile-causing,
exile-ending God has moved decisively outside predictable
expectations.

2. It does not surprise us that Jeremiah, a child of Deuteronomy, should articulate the same divine step, only in
more lyrical form. Jeremiah of course knows the old Torah.
He knows that in Deuteronomy 24:1-4 Moses declared, in
good patriarchal fashion, that a woman who leaves her husband and goes to a second failed marriage cannot go back to
her first husband. But Jeremiah, a poet pushed to extremity
by circumstance, takes up the old commandment and knows
that something new and out of bounds must be said.[11] Now, in
poetic imagination, Yhwh is the first husband, Baal is the second husband, and Israel is sleeping from husband to husband,
all, to be sure, in patriarchal casting. But now the God who
reaches beyond invites her back. "Softly and tenderly Jesus is
calling, 'Come home . . .'":

> Return, faithless Israel, says the Lord.
> I will not look on you in anger,
> for I am merciful, says the Lord . . .
> Return, O faithless children, says the Lord . . .

> and I will bring you to Zion . . .
> Return, O faithless children,
> I will heal your faithlessness. (Jer 3:12, 14, 22)

And then the specificity:

> If you return, O Israel, says the Lord,
> if you return to me,
> if you remove your abominations from my presence,
> and do not waver,
> and if you swear, "As the Lord lives!"
> in truth, in justice, and in uprightness [i.e., righteousness],
> then nations shall be blessed by him,
> and by him they shall boast. (4:1-2)

We get yet again the old terms of fidelity: *amunah, mispat, yasar,* all the requirements of the old Torah tradition. The poem would have us recognize that Yhwh is willing to violate (or forego) even Yhwh's own Torah for the sake of the relationship. The second chance is grounded in Yhwh's readiness to violate Torah for a homecoming and a renewal of relationship.

3. Even Ezekiel, in his priestly symmetrical reasoning, can imagine Yhwh's capacity to reach beyond. He lines out three men, father King Josiah, son King Jehoiakim, and grandson King Jehoiachin.[12] The righteous father will live in his Torah obedience. The son, a violent shedder of blood, will die in his iniquity. And the grandson, the exiled boy king in Babylon, continues to be privileged in his righteousness amid the long history of violation by his family, his city, and his people.

For all of his tenacious symmetry, Ezekiel must go further than symmetry. He dares to imagine that the chain of guilt and punishment can be broken. He does not say how it is broken. But he knows:

> The righteousness of the righteous shall be his own, and the wickedness of the wicked shall be his own. (18:20)

The grandson need not be encumbered by ancient abominations, but need only embrace the ways of covenant:

But if the wicked turn away from all their sins that they have committed and keep all my statutes and do what is lawful and right, they shall surely live; they shall not die. None of the transgressions that they have committed shall be remembered against them; for the righteousness that they have done they shall live. (vv. 21-22)

And then the ultimate declaration of Ezekiel on the mercy of God:

Have I any pleasure in the death of the wicked, says the Lord God, and not rather that they should turn from their ways and live? (v. 23)

This is not a God who wants to operate within the heavy sanctions of common theology. This is an uncommon God who wills an uncommon possibility for an uncommon people. This God wills life. And so the prophet will have God repeat it one more time as a conclusion:

For I have no pleasure in the death of anyone, says the Lord God. Turn, then, and live. (v. 32)

It is about a turn back to covenant, back to Torah, back to fidelity.

4. Isaiah in the exile will not have it differently. For all the good news of exilic Isaiah, it is about the turn:

Seek the Lord while he may be found,
call upon him while he is near;
let the wicked forsake their way,
and the unrighteous their thoughts;
let them return to the Lord, that he may have mercy on them,
and to our God, for he will abundantly pardon. (55:6-7)

I read this as directed to a community that has expressly given in to Babylonian reality and now is summoned to reengage the particularities of Israelite Torah obedience. The turn, as in Deuteronomy, finds mercy at the other end. And now the word is uttered: "pardon!"[13] What an extraordinary moment in the life of this dislocated people, that the God of grace who occupies exile makes a way out of no way:

> For my thoughts are not your thoughts,
> nor are your ways my ways, says the Lord.
> For as the heavens are higher than the earth,
> so are my ways higher than your ways
> and my thoughts than your thoughts. (vv. 8-9)

It is astonishing that the summons to return that now brackets Deuteronomic Torah in Deuteronomy 4 and 30 should turn up all over exile:

- In Jeremiah: Return, O faithless children, I will heal your faithlessness (3:22).
- In Ezekiel: Turn, then, and live (18:32).
- In Isaiah: Let them return to the Lord, that he may have mercy (55:7).

It is as though Yhwh had been reading Yhwh's memos about justice as transformative relation. The justice of Yhwh is not about common quid pro quo. Covenantal justice operates with a surplus grounded in abundant generosity. Israel knew this from the challenge of maintaining a social neighborliness that is only possible with such surplus. It is the same awareness at which we are always arriving out of a context of rigorous parsimony that makes neighborliness impossible. They found that necessary practice of surplus rooted in the readiness of the creator God to enact such surplus. This justice is about a reach past predictable, uncompromising sanctions to restoration. Thus, commutative justice is transposed into restorative justice. Yhwh's way is indeed restorative justice writ large . . . or, if you prefer, grace, "grace in the wilderness," grace in venues of despair and helplessness and hopelessness, by the God who invites all back to fidelity.

5. It does not surprise us that what is writ large in Israel's public life according to the prophets should find echo and parallel in more intimate contexts of personal tribulation. The

whole world of lament and thanks is a world of the divine reach beyond symmetry. In Psalm 32 the speaker knows that alienation from God causes psychosomatic symptoms:

> While I kept silence, my body wasted away
> through my groaning all day long.
> For day and night your hand was heavy upon me;
> my strength was dried up as by the heat of summer. (vv. 3-4)

That diagnosis, however, is followed by the dramatic "then" of restoration:

> Then I acknowledged my sin to you,
> and I did not hide my iniquity;
> I said, "I will confess my transgressions to the Lord,"
> and you forgave the guilt of my sin. (v. 5)

I confessed . . . you forgave! No pause, no hesitation, only total readiness:

> You are a hiding place for me;
> you preserved me from trouble;
> you surround me with glad cries of deliverance. (v. 7)

Israel can pray boldly with insistence, because it knows that the one addressed reaches beyond:

> Be gracious to me, O Lord, for I am languishing;
> O Lord, heal me, for my bones are shaking with terror . . .
> Turn, O Lord, save my life;
> deliver me for the sake of your steadfast love. (6:2, 4)

And then restoration:

> The Lord has heard the sound of my weeping.
> The Lord has heard my supplication;
> the Lord accepts my prayer. (vv. 8-9)

Israel in exile, Israelites in languishing desolation, have no recourse except back to the God of fidelity. It is, every time, a high-risk prayer. But it is characteristically a prayer received: Yhwh heard, Yhwh accepts!

Or the pastoral emergency goes public, as in Psalm 107:

> Some were sick through their sinful ways,
> and because of their iniquities endured affliction;
> they loathed any kind of food,
> and they drew near to the gates of death. (vv. 17-18)

But Israel by now knows what to do: "They cried." And then, without pause or punctuation:

> He saved them from their distress;
> he sent out his word and healed them,
> and delivered them from destruction. (vv. 19-20)

It was, as it is every time, a wonder, a wondrous work, an inexplicable transformation that is sealed by a work of gratitude. So also the speaker, in Psalm 35, knows the right response to the divine reach of a second chance:

> *Then* my soul shall rejoice in the Lord,
> exulting in his deliverance . . .
> *Then* I will thank you in the great congregation;
> in the mighty throng I will praise you . . .
> *Then* my tongue shall tell of your righteousness
> and of your praise all day long. (vv. 9, 18, 28)

This is the threefold "then" of full restoration.

III.

The God of second chances is fully *receptive* to Israel's turn. In the depth of dismay, however, Israel came to understand that the God of second chances is not just receptive. The God of second chances beyond every chance is an *active agent* who does not wait on Israel's return, because that wait may be very long indeed. God will not wait, but reaches out beyond the symmetry of common theology for restored relationship. God will violate God's best judgment in an inexplicable initiative.

1. In Hosea 11, the choicest text of them all, there is no return by Israel. There is only a tirade by God who then catches Godself in mid-sentence and reverses field. The reversal is evoked not by Israel but by Yhwh's own self. The poet gives us access to God's internal life, wherein Yhwh struggles with a common theology that issues in harsh judgments. Yhwh has a readiness, on occasion, to violate that common theology for a way that enacts Yhwh's yearning for durable fidelity. Yhwh interrupts the tirade (vv. 5-7) with critical self-reflection:

> How can I give you up, Ephraim?
> How can I hand you over, O Israel?
> How can I make you like Admah?
> How can I treat you like Zeboiim? (v. 8)

And then fresh divine resolve:

> My heart recoils within me;
> my compassion grows warm and tender.
> I will not execute my fierce anger;
> I will not again destroy Ephraim;
> For I am God and no mortal,
> the Holy One in your midst,
> and I will not come in wrath. (vv. 8-9)

This is no ordinary God. This is the Holy One. But this Holy One is not remote in the heavens or in the temple. This Holy One is in your midst, in the midst enough to notice the fracture, in the midst enough to care, in the midst enough to reach. It is this reach into the wilderness that makes possible the poem with which we began:

> *Therefore* I will now allure her,
> and bring her into the wilderness,
> and speak tenderly to her. (2:14)

It is this reach, against all propriety, that permits the God of Hosea to declare:

> I will take you for my wife in righteousness and in justice, in steadfast love and in mercy. (v. 19)

2. It is two centuries after Hosea before the texts of the inexplicable divine reach begins to cluster. This cluster comes to voice in the exile, in the venue of abandonment and despair.

So Jeremiah, with the promise of new covenant. No warrant is given for new covenant. It is simply unilateral:

> I will make a new covenant with the house of Israel and with the house of Judah. (31:31)

In this remarkable text we have been excessively preoccupied with "New Covenant" and the different claims of Jews and Christians, so that we have not often enough noticed the final remarkable promise to Israel:

> For I will forgive their iniquity, and remember their sin no more. (v. 34)

Now the word is uttered: "Forgive." Forgive and forget (do not remember!). It is unilateral and unconditional. This is the deepest, fullest disclosure of God's capacity and God's intention. In the wilderness of displacement, the grace of newness is performed.

Notice how different this is from Jeremiah 3–4, which is permeated with a bid for "return." Here there is no summons to return, as though it is not required or as though it is not possible, for this defiant Israel can no more change its recalcitrance than a leopard will change its spots (13:23). Yhwh's realism about Israel is not unlike Yhwh's realism about humanity in the flood narrative. At the beginning and at the end of the flood narrative, human imagination is distorted (Gen 6; 8:21). No change there! But Yhwh has changed from the relentless God of common theology to the covenant-making, promise-presiding God of grace. So Israel: "We have sinned . . . from our youth" (Jer 3:25; see Gen 8:21). But Yhwh will not despair, because Yhwh has resources for a second chance, the chance for a people helplessly in exile. No return, no whisper of expectation from God, only "I will forgive." The offer of forgiveness is seconded by the Jeremiah tradition in chapter 33:

> I will restore the fortunes of Judah and the fortunes of Israel, and rebuild them as they were at first. I will cleanse them of all the guilt of their sin against me, and I will

forgive all the guilt of their sin and rebellion against me. . . .
They shall fear and tremble because of all the good and all
the prosperity I provide for it. (vv. 7-9)

"Restore fortunes" is a catchword for the new possibility in
Jeremiah. The outcome will be "all the good that I do for
them" (v. 9) issuing in joy. At the center, now a second time,
is "forgive":

"I will cleanse," a salute to the priestly tradition;

"I will forgive," a break with prophetic speeches of
judgment.

The chapter goes on with rebuilding and rejoicing.

3. In the famous text of chapter 18, Ezekiel (and Yhwh)
had relied on the "turn" of Israel: "Turn, then, and live." But
even in the hardnosed reflection of Ezekiel, Yhwh will not
wait for the turn. In the elongated promises of chapters 34,
36, and 37, it is all first-person declaration. In chapter 34, after
the failure of Judean kings, this God will now enact direct rule
and be king and do kingly things for Israel:

I myself will be the shepherd of my sheep, and I will make
them lie down, says the Lord God. I will seek the lost, and
I will bring back the strayed, and I will bind up the injured,
and I will strengthen the weak, but the fat and the strong I
will destroy. I will feed them with justice. (vv. 15-16)

It will come down to justice, justice in the negative for the
fat and strong, justice and restoration for the vulnerable and
resourceless. In chapter 37, after a query about the future that
Ezekiel cannot answer, there is this intense divine resolve
about restoration:

I am going to open your graves, and bring you up from your
graves, O my people; and I will bring you back to the land of
Israel. And you shall know that I am the Lord, when I open
your graves, and bring you up from your graves, O my people. I will put my spirit within you, and you shall live, and I
will place you on your own soil; then you shall know that I,
the Lord, have spoken and will act, says the Lord. (vv. 14-16)

This is the reach of divine grace that defies the deathliness of Babylon and that makes new life possible.

In chapter 36 as well, there is no more waiting for the turn from Israel. Now it is all first-person resolve:

> I will take you from the nations, and gather you from all the countries, and bring you into your own land. I will sprinkle clean water upon you, and you shall be clean from all your uncleannesses, and from all your idols I will cleanse you. A new heart I will give you, and a new spirit I will put within you; and I will remove from your body the heart of stone and give you a heart of flesh. (vv. 24-26)[14]

But Ezekiel, quite remarkably, offers a daring grounding for the gracious reach of newness. This promissory paragraph is framed at the beginning and at the end in this way:

> It is not for your sake, O house of Israel, that I am about to act, but for the sake of my holy name, which you have profaned among the nations to which you came.... It is not for your sake that I will act, says the Lord God; let that be known to you. (vv. 22, 32)

This God is no softie, no cream puff, no good buddy. This God, the one offended by Israel's abomination, is filled with intense self-regard. Israel, in its sordidness, has diminished Yhwh's reputation among the nations. And now Yhwh will act in self-repair to restore the good holy name. That, however, can be only accomplished finally by a restoration of Israel, so that all the nations can see the faithful power of Yhwh. It is, I judge, astonishing that Yhwh, in Ezekiel, does not consider recovery of reputation simply by scattering Israel or by throwing Israel under the Babylonian bus. No, even the high-handed Holy One in Ezekiel cannot scuttle Israel, and so must restore Israel in order to restore self. This is not a very attractive portrayal of grace; it is, however, a deeply resolved portrayal of grace, for God's own well-being depends upon this act toward Israel. Perhaps this is why God so loved the world, because this God is linked inexplicably to the world the way God is

linked inexplicably to Israel. And so the promises here move
to irreducible assurances grounded in divine self-regard:

> I will make a covenant of peace with them; it shall be an
> everlasting covenant with them, and I will bless them and
> multiply them, and will set my sanctuary among them for-
> ever. (37:26-27)

4. So it is as well with Isaiah in the exile. We have seen
the summons to repent in chapter 55. Those verses host a turn
as a condition of pardon. In chapter 54, however, the matter
is very different. Here Yhwh engages in self-reflection about
the failed linkage to Israel. In patriarchal imagery, Israel goes
quickly in the chapter from fruitful mother to shamed widow:

> Like a wife forsaken and grieved in spirit,
> Like the wife of a man's youth when she is cast off. (v. 6)

It is as though the poet ruminates on the harsh fate of this
abandoned, scorned woman in exile. No, it is more like Yhwh
engaging in reflection on the harsh outcome of displacement.
This powerful reflection yields a new divine resolve. It is not
quite a divine apology; but it is a divine admission, perhaps the
most remarkable one in Scripture. God finally is able to say
upon reflection:

> For a brief moment I abandoned you . . .
> In overflowing wrath for a moment I hid my face from
> you. (vv. 7-8)

The term "abandon" is about divorce. It is the same word we
know in the Gospel quote from Psalm 22, "Why have you for-
saken?" Here there is no renunciation of Israel, no reprimand
or scolding. Here there is only recognition of "my" role in this
sorry state of affairs. It is as though the first line of each of
these two verses leads to a quite fresh and unexpected resolve:

> But with great compassion I will gather you. . . .
> But with everlasting love I will have compassion on you,
> says the Lord your redeemer. (vv. 7, 8)

The two verses deeply intertwine divine admission and divine resolve. Two times there is divine admission; two times there is rhetorical reversal. Twice there is compassion, first "great compassion" that leads to homecoming, second "in overflowing love." We are left to wonder how it was that the poet could dare to host such a line of divine decision-making. More than that, we are left to pause over this revolution in God's own heart. This is, to be sure, a God of overflowing wrath. But more than that! This is a kind of self-critical reflection that permits Yhwh to act in a "better self" toward Israel, whether Israel seeks to return or not. Divine compassion is the order of the day.

5. What pertains in the national epic of Israel operates as well in the intimacy of the Psalter. The Psalms do not shrink from divine abuse and divine neglect. Pressed deeper, however, the psalmists know better. Thus, in the well-beloved Psalm 103, we get a reiteration of the great catalogue of fidelity:

> The Lord is merciful and gracious,
> slow to anger and abounding in steadfast love. (v. 8)

And then an assurance that is reminiscent of Isaiah 54:

> He will not always accuse,
> nor will he keep his anger forever.
> He does not deal with us according to our sins,
> nor repay us according to our iniquities.
> For as the heavens are high above the earth,
> so great is his steadfast love toward those who fear him;
> as far as the east is from the west,
> so far he removes our transgressions from us. (vv. 9-12)

And that assurance is seconded by a double use of "compassion":

> As a father has compassion for his children,
> so the Lord has compassion for those who fear him. (v. 13)

The psalm does not deny the harshness of God's anger in a mode of common theology. But the anger ebbs. What endures is the true self of God in God's characteristic self-disclosure:

. . . who forgives all your iniquities,
who heals all your diseases,
who redeems your life from the Pit,
who crowns you with steadfast love and mercy,
who satisfies you with good as long as you live. (vv. 3-5)

This conviction of God's true self becomes the ground for petition, as in Psalm 86. This is petition based not on repentance but only in need:

For you, O Lord, are good and forgiving,
Abounding in steadfast love to all who call on you . . .
But you, O Lord, are a God merciful and gracious,
Slow to anger and abounding in steadfast love and faithfulness.
    (vv. 5, 15)

And from this a torrent of imperatives:

Incline your ear, O Lord, and answer me . . .
Preserve my life . . .
Gladden the soul of your servant . . .
Listen to my cry of supplication . . .
Turn to me and be gracious to me;
give strength to your servant;
save the child of your serving girl . . .
Show me a sign of your favor. (vv. 1, 2, 4, 6, 16, 17)

The testimony is everywhere, evoked as it is by the wilderness of deep need and forlornness. There is everywhere a bid that Israel should want this relation enough to return. This God is indeed like a parent who waits on a teenager to repent, and falls asleep waiting, or, better, stays awake all night waiting. And then, finally, cannot wait any longer, and yields with a free embrace:

As a father has compassion for his children,
so the Lord has compassion for those who fear him. (103:13)

This is a father who swirls in an eddy of compassion. This is a mother who carries the child in womblike mother love:

Can a woman forget her nursing child,
or show no compassion for the child of her womb?
Even these may forget,
yet I will not forget you. (Isa 49:15)

It is that father, this mother, who meets the desolate in transformative resolve.

IV.

The wilderness is the proper venue for the exhibit of Yhwh's
grace. It did not take long, however, for Israel to recognize
that *the God of second chances*, attested by prophets and poets,
is also *the God of first chances*. This God not only intervenes in
wilderness failures but also initiates at the outset and sustains
both Israel and the world, so that it is all a distinctive performance of divine grace. This is the inescapable reach that "calls
into existence things that do not exist" (Rom 4:17).

Israel reflected on its own life, the way in which we might
reflect on our baptism. Israel saw that its very existence was a
consequence of the inexplicable reach of Yhwh into the undif-
ferentiated world of many peoples. The origin and destiny of
Israel, so they recognized, was not possible, except for the
reach of Yhwh. The family of Terah, so they remembered, was
mired from the first in defeat. Sarah was barren; Abraham was
without a future (Gen 11:30). And God spoke! God declared,
"Go; I will bless you." The one who speaks is the creator God
who now creates a *novum* in human history. The force of blessing works its way through the narrative until the ambiguous
claim of the Joseph narrative. Joseph, it turned out, was a ren-
egade who signed on with Pharaoh. Before that, however, he
declared to his astonished brothers:

> God sent me before you to preserve life. . . . God sent me
> before you to preserve for you a remnant on the earth, and
> to keep alive for you many survivors. (Gen 45:5, 7)

In the end the narrator can have Joseph judge of the dangerous vagaries of his narrative that "God intended it for good"

(50:20). This is the God who provides. This is the people for whom God provides. This is the God of inexplicable provision. This is the God who operates providentially in the life of this people.

It is this generous, inexplicable graciousness toward the family of Abraham that surfaces, in the final form of the text, in the Exodus narrative. That narrative begins in the desperate cry of the oppressed in slavery (Exod 2:23). The beginning is a bodily cry of the unbearable, a cry addressed to no one in particular. Except of course, "their cry for help rose up to God" (2:23). And God focused on that ragtag "mixed multitude" (12:38). It is thought by some interpreters, as you know, that the ancestral narratives of Genesis and the Exodus narrative have been joined only later in the tradition. Maybe so—but even if so, the connection is first made by the God who propels the text. So it is that "God saw, God heard, God knew, God remembered." Astonishing that when God looked on this nondescript company of sufferers, God was reminded of the family line of Genesis. They did not look at all alike. It is the dense risk of fidelity and imagination that lets this company of nobodies without merit or qualification be cast as the chosen. It is simply astonishing that God can say of this uncredentialed company, "Israel is my firstborn son" (4:22). God saw what no one else saw. Or God delivered and made it so. Either way, the divine reach "called into existence what had not until now existed."

The rest is history. But such a peculiar history! It is the history of emancipation that made a future possible, for Pharaoh was not into generating futures. It is a history and a future that depended upon the wind, wind that operates for emancipation, wind that forecloses the control of Pharaoh:

> The Lord drove the sea back by a strong east wind all night, and turned the sea into dry land; and the waters were divided. The Israelites went into the sea on dry ground, the waters forming a wall for them on their right and on their

left. . . . Then the Lord said to Moses, "Stretch out your hand over the sea, so that the water may come back upon the Egyptians, upon their chariots and chariot drivers." . . . The sea returned to its normal depth. (Exod 14:21-22, 26-27)

Of course the critics used to "explain" this wind; and now the critics say it could not have happened, critics who want to turn the wonder of grace into explanatory categories. But of course Israel defies these critics with its liturgical passion concerning the one who

brought Israel out from among them,
for his steadfast love endures forever;
with a strong hand and an outstretched arm,
for his steadfast love endures forever;
who divided the Red Sea in two,
for his steadfast love endures forever;
and made Israel pass through the midst of it,
for his steadfast love endures forever;
but overthrew Pharaoh and his army in the Red Sea,
for his steadfast love endures forever. (Ps 136:11-15)

It is the divine reach, in the telling of Israel, that overrides the ferocious power of Pharaoh and makes life possible.

It is no wonder that in these two tales of beginning, with an utterance to Abraham and Sarah, with a wind against Pharaoh, Israel was compelled to accept a verdict of divine grace as the only source of life. So in Deuteronomy, Israel's narrative exposition of the inexplicable, Israel could declare:

For you are a people holy to the Lord your God; the Lord your God has chosen you out of all the peoples on earth to be his people, his treasured possession. (7:6-7)

When the Lord your God thrusts them out before you, do not say to yourself, "It is because of my righteousness that the Lord has brought me in to occupy this land. . . . It is not because of your righteousness or the uprightness of your heart that you are going in to occupy the land." (9:4-5)

> Yet the Lord set his heart in love on your ancestors alone
> and chose you, their descendants after them, out of all the
> peoples, as it is today. (10:15)

It could not be more elemental than this: "God set his heart
on you and chose you." The verb suggests desire for, eagerness
that moves in the direction of lust. God wanted you and wants
you. To be sure, the tradition of Deuteronomy cannot resist
turning this gracious initiative into warning about disobedience. More than that, the declaration of chosenness has a per-
nicious side of destructiveness, both in the ancient text and
in contemporary usage.[15] None of that, however, mitigates the
wonder of the first chance, a first chance performed by divine
affection and by the wind that blesses the world, making it
open enough to begin again.

The God of second chances creates possibilities where
there were none. But behind second chances are first chances.
When Israel reflected on the future-permitting wind of God,
it dared to appropriate the great Near Eastern myths of creation. It linked the miracle of its own existence to the miracle
of the world, also wrought by this same God. The doxologies of
creation are articulations of God's grace. Israel knew from the
outset that the world is not autonomous, not self-generating or
self-sustaining. Thus it could dare to say:

> By the word of the Lord the heavens were made,
> and all their host by the breath of his mouth.
> He gathered the waters of the sea as in a bottle;
> he put the deeps in storehouses. . . .
> He spoke, and it came to be;
> he commanded, and it stood firm. (Ps 33:6-7, 9)

It is only utterance; it is all "fresh from the word." The world
itself summons to awe:

> O Lord my God, when I in awesome wonder
> consider all the worlds thy hands have made . . .
> Then sings my soul, my Savior God to thee,
> How great thou art![16]

More than that:

> He loves righteousness and justice;
> the earth is full of the steadfast love of the Lord. (Ps 33:5)

A pondering of creation brings us back to the great terms of fidelity: *sedeqah*, *mispat*, and *hesed*, ordained in the very fabric of creation.

Or, more fully, Psalm 104, in doxological awe, moves from the expanse of the foundation of the earth, all the way through abundant waters that are given in an acutely arid climate, to the rhythm of day and night, night for lion work, day for human work (vv. 2-23). The recital lasts a while as the divine name is deliberately withheld; Israel fearlessly engages in "natural theology." But then the divine name bursts out in verse 24, "O Lord!"—"O wow!"

> O Lord, how manifold are your works! (v. 24)

Israel knows that the grace of reliable food must evoke thanks:

> These all look to you to give them their food in due season;
> when you give it to them, they gather it up;
> when you open your hand, they are filled with good things.
>   (vv. 27-28)

Israel knows about the force of the wind that becomes the substance of breath:

> You make the clouds your chariot,
> you ride on the wings of the wind,
> you make the winds your messengers,
> Fire and flame your ministers. (vv. 3-4)

But then, by verse 29, that wind is the source of life:

> When you hide your face, they are dismayed;
> when you take away their breath, they die and return to
>   their dust.
> When you send forth your spirit, they are created;
> and you renew the face of the ground. (vv. 29-30)

It is all wind, all *ruah*, all freely given vitality, all inscrutable, the holy reach that makes life possible. It is no wonder that

at the very outset, it is *wind-spirit-breath* (this baffles transla-
tors) that hovers and makes life possible (Gen 1:2). How else to
articulate the originary grace that stands behind the life of the
world? Thus, "first chance" is a meditation on the wind that
blows back the waters of chaos, on the wind that blew back the
Red Sea, on the wind that operates like a great iron lung for
the world, wind that will eventually propel the church, wind
that blows where it will:

> The wind blows where it chooses, and you hear the sound
> of it, but you do not know where it comes from or where
> it goes. So it is with everyone who is born of the Spirit.
> (John 3:8)

The world, Israel, and eventually the church are born of the
Spirit,

> who by understanding made the heavens,
> for his steadfast love endures forever;
> who spread out the earth on the waters,
> for his steadfast love endures forever;
> who made the great lights,
> for his steadfast love endures forever;
> the sun to rule over the day,
> for his steadfast love endures forever;
> the moon and stars to rule over the night,
> for his steadfast love endures forever. (Ps 136:5-9)

It is all marked by an initiating, sustaining wind of *hesed*. There
were no chances for creation or for Israel that were pre-wind
or pre-*hesed*! That is the first chance attested in the tradition
of this second-chance people.

V.

Israel's break with common theology was a recognition, first,
that Yhwh was receptive to Israel's "turn," and second, that
Yhwh, without waiting, would actively engage in the restoration of Israel. Because God's work is all saturated with *hesed*
and because the wind-giving God loves *mispat* and *sedeqah*,

there is no chance of settling for common theology of quid pro quo sanctions. And yet Israel, after its "mutations" of common theology, if it is to live in the world, must return to common theology.[17] It does so, however, with an altered perception and passion. Common theology, which always leads to domination, now is deeply deconstructed by the reach of divine grace. To use my own language, now this "structure legitimation" practice has "embraced pain."[18] Israel returns to common theology, having had its pain embraced in a second chance, second chance of rescue from Egypt, second chance of forgiveness in exile, second chance of deliverance from the helplessness of the pit. And so Israel now "legitimates structure" differently in light of "pain embraced." Does it stagger you as it does me, that in the long broad sweep of politics in our society, it has been Jews who have been relentlessly committed to a practice of justice . . . surely because Jews actively process the long pained history of Sinai and its emancipation?

It occurs to me that the last part of the book of Isaiah is about legitimating structure after having embraced pain.[19] The book of Isaiah knows about deliverance from exile; in the wake of that deliverance the poet is able to imagine a different divine governance, one of justice born of grace. At the outset, so-called Third Isaiah declares its agenda:

> Maintain justice, and do what is right,
> for soon my salvation will come,
> and my deliverance be revealed. (56:1)

It is all about *mispat*, but now justice is performed in generosity. It comes out this way:

1. In chapter 56, in an argument about inclusion and exclusion, about who is a real Jew, the text makes room for eunuchs and foreigners, the very "other" that would threaten tribal order. But new governance is a governance of welcome:

> These I will bring to my holy mountain . . .
> for my house shall be called a house of prayer for all peo-
>   ples. (v. 7)

And then a rumination about "gathering" and homecoming, and this in the face of a world culture that wants to "scatter" all "others" to oblivion:

> Thus says the Lord God,
> who gathers the outcasts of Israel,
> I will gather others to them besides those already gath-
> ered. (v. 8)

Following after the God who gathers, this community becomes one of welcome.

2. In Isaiah 58 we are offered a fresh formulation of authentic worship. The lines are familiar to us, so familiar that we may not notice their radicality:

> Is not this the fast that I choose:
> to loose the bonds of injustice,
> to undo the thongs of the yoke,
> to let the oppressed go free,
> and to break every yoke?
> Is it not to share your bread with the hungry,
> and bring the homeless poor into your house;
> when you see the naked to cover them,
> and not to hide yourself from your own kin? (vv. 6-7)

It turns out that the others—the oppressed, the hungry, the homeless poor, the naked—are kinfolk . . . our own flesh. Here is a catalogue of the others who threaten, the excluded, those left behind, those dreaded as non-producers. Indeed, this inventory anticipates the company of those with whom we may inherit the kingdom in Matthew 25:34-36.

In the Isaiah text, moreover, the summons to a new righteousness is in the context of the phony worship of those who love to perform piety while they serve their own interests and oppress workers. Who knew that common theology would be able to raise the question of minimum wage, because the reach of grace reaches into the economy?

3. In the more familiar Isaiah 61, "structure legitimation" that has "embraced pain" comes back to the wind. It is that wind of the Lord God who blows to new vocation and to new historical possibility. You know the words:

> The spirit of the Lord God is upon me,
> because the Lord has anointed me;
> he has sent me to bring good news to the oppressed,
> to bind up the brokenhearted,
> to proclaim liberty to the captives,
> and release to the prisoners;
> to proclaim the year of the Lord's favor,
> and the day of vengeance of our God. (vv. 1-2)

No doubt in that world as in ours, prisoners are the ones in lockdown because they were ill-connected and could not afford a good lawyer. Like now, lockdown was for those who owed debts to society, the debt they could not pay, the debt and duty of endless productivity. Of course it is an anachronism to reason so. But still, if this text is about Jubilee—"the year of the Lord's favor"—it is new economic policy wrought as an act of grace, with debts forgiven, life restored for those left behind, loans adjusted, all in a form of neighborliness.

The poem declares that those who follow the lead of the wind will transform society:

> Garland instead of ashes,
> the oil of gladness instead of mourning,
> the mantle of praise instead of a faint spirit.
> They shall be called oaks of righteousness,
> the planting of the Lord, to display his glory.
> They shall build up the ancient ruins,
> they shall raise up the former devastations;
> they shall repair the ruined cities,
> the devastations of many generations. (vv. 3-4)

What a mandate: "plant, build up, raise up, repair!" None of that work can be done on the basis of anxious quid pro quo.

All of it can be done, so the text anticipates, by the propulsion of the wind among those who are back from exile for a second chance. The work of those who are ready for a second chance is to offer a first chance to those who have not yet had that first chance. Policy is the place where the divine reach of grace will have its say!

It is no wonder, back in Nazareth, that when they understood Jesus' meaning in his reading of Isaiah 61, they wanted to eliminate him (Luke 4:28-29). Of course ordinary common theology has no place for the gracious slippage of a reach beyond quid pro quo. But Israel, in its post-exile rescue, can imagine that even policy may reflect the pathos-filled purpose of Yhwh, the one who "forgives, heals, redeems, crowns, and satisfies" (Ps 103:3-5). Imagine that these terms of divine reach now concern public policy and practice: forgive, heal, redeem, crown, satisfy! It is a plethora of transformative goodness that now marks the body politic.

VI.

The grace of God marks the abundance of the world, the well-being of Israel, the practice of public policy, and the dispatch of persons in their capacity to form and sustain a viable human community in the interest of the common good. We have seen the way in which the grace of Yhwh transposes "commutative" justice into restorative justice.[20]

While we have focused on the agency and character of Yhwh, we conclude with two reflections on the ways in which that grace is received in the creaturely life of the world. On the one hand, God's grace situated in creatureliness yields a beauty that makes the creation "good." As Claus Westermann has suggested, the verdict of the sixth day of creation, "very good," is an aesthetic judgment, "very beautiful."[21] That beauty, moreover, is fully, even extravagantly celebrated in the love poetry of the Song of Solomon:

How beautiful are you, my love, how very beautiful!
Your eyes are doves behind your veil.
Your hair is like a flock of goats,
moving down the slopes of Gilead.
Your teeth are like a flock of shorn ewes
that have come up from the washing,
all of which bear twins,
and not one among them is bereaved.
Your lips are like a crimson thread,
and your mouth is lovely.
Your cheeks are like halves of a pomegranate
behind your veil.
Your neck is like the tower of David,
built in courses;
on it hang a thousand bucklers,
all of them shields of warriors.
Your two breasts are like two fawns,
twins of a gazelle, that feed among the lilies. (4:1-7)

Bonhoeffer has proposed that this poetry is the best creation theology we have in the Old Testament, attesting to both the bodily gracefulness of the creature and the capacity for beauty of human speech.[22] The poem can linger in the detail of bodily beauty, so that grace comes not only as graciousness but as *gracefulness*, a way of being in freedom that is unhindered by fear and unimpeded by any anxious shame.

On the other hand, the graciousness of Yhwh is ethical, an ethical performance by those who have fully received graciousness. The move from Yhwh's graciousness to human (Israelite) graciousness is neatly expressed in Deuteronomy 10:17-19. The doxology of Moses begins in a grand royal cadence:

> For the Lord our God is God of gods and Lord of lords, the great God, mighty and awesome.

Bur then, in midsentence, the rhetoric devolves from heavenly grandeur to political economy. It is this all-presiding God who will undertake economic rehabilitation in the form of restorative justice:

> . . . who is not partial and takes no bribe, who executes justice for the orphan and the widow, who loves the strangers, providing them food and clothing. (vv. 17-18)

The graciousness of Yhwh takes on quotidian dimension with food and clothing pertaining to the familiar triad of vulnerability, the widow, orphan, and stranger. The divine descent is a reach into mundane reality. And then, immediately, the doxological affirmation of Moses turns to imperative summons:

> You shall also love the stranger, for you were strangers in the land of Egypt. (v. 19)

It is common to translate the third term in the recurring triad as "immigrant." But likely the rendering here in the NRSV is more poignant: "stranger," the "other" who may appear as threat or rival. This succinct mandate articulates in most radical form the reach of grace to be practiced in the political economy: "love the stranger." The appeal to the Exodus suggests that Yhwh's initial engagement on behalf of Israel was exactly a radical reach that is now to be replicated in the action of Israel.

We may suggest a simple typology for the imperatives of divine grace:

- Reach for *the neighbor*.
- Reach for *the stranger*.
- Reach for *the enemy*.

Israel is of course enjoined to love *the neighbor* (Lev 19:17-18). That in itself is a serious demand, because the neighbor may also be experienced as threat or as competitor. But Israel, recipient of Yhwh's grace, is to commit graciousness toward the neighbor. Second, Israel is mandated to "love *the stranger*." Or in Leviticus 19:33-35, the NRSV renders the term as "alien":

> You shall not oppress the alien. The alien who resides with
> you shall be to you as the citizen among you; you shall love
> the alien as yourself, for you were aliens in the land of Egypt:
> I am the Lord your God.

The mandate here is as in Deuteronomy 10:19. And of course,
with the stranger (immigrant, alien) characteristically come
widow and orphan, so that grace is performed as an economic
act of neighborly welfare toward those who are not yet neighbor (see Deut 24:17-22).

Third, love *your enemy*. Ancient Israel does not quite reach
there; that reach is the verdict of the later Sermon on the
Mount (Matt 5:43-48). But that reach from *neighbor* to *stranger*
is already well on its way to *enemy* as well. All social relationships are transformed by the awareness that Yhwh's grace in
the second chance and Yhwh's grace in the first chance give
Israel many chances to be different in social relationships. In
a world of such divinely given chances, social relationships are
never quid pro quo; they are marked by a reach beyond that
becomes an ethic of grace. Thus, concerning the righteous:

> They are gracious, merciful, and righteous. (Ps 112:4)[23]

That grace was already tilted toward the economy with the
gifts of food and clothing given to the stranger by the God of
gods and Lord of lords. Thus, human performance of graciousness concerns:

- Lending generously (Ps 112:5).
- Conducting affairs in justice (v. 5).
- Freely distributing to the poor (v. 9).

The righteous can never practice justice without the reach
beyond in policy and in practice that aids the recovery
of the neighborhood. Reception of God's grace propels
neighborhood-creating gracefulness.

4

LAW
The Summons to Keep Listening

In what is arguably the latest book in the Old Testament, the seer Daniel carefully negotiates his Jewish faith amid the Persians. In the extended narrative of Daniel 6, his Jewish piety collides with Persian governance. Daniel is a respected, successful imperial "president" to whom the Persian satraps report; his task is to protect the interests of the king. He is so successful that the king plans to "appoint him over the whole kingdom," an appointment that evokes jealousy and hostility among the other officers (v. 3). Daniel, however, cannot be charged with negligence or corruption, because he is so loyal to the king. His detractors, however, plan to trip him up over his piety that lives in tension with Persian rule:

> We shall not find any ground for complaint against this Daniel unless we find it in connection with the law of his God. (v. 5)

And of course their plot works, because they persuade the king, Darius, to make a rule that precludes prayer to any but to "you, O king." The penalty will be execution at the hands of lions.

I.

Thus, the issue is joined. Darius promulgates "the law of the Medes and the Persians" that cannot be changed (v. 12). The conspirators aim to catch Daniel out because he obeys the "law of his God" (v. 5). It is "the law of the Medes and the Persians" versus "the law of his God." It is law versus law, an interface that poses all the crucial questions about law. These two laws are of course in tension because each of them commands an exclusive loyalty: the "law of his God" commands prayers to the Jewish God of the Exodus; the law of the Medes and the Persians commands worship only of the Persian king. Daniel the Jew faces the impossible choice of which law to obey, which God to address in prayer. But there is one other defining difference between these two "laws." The law of the Medes and the Persians cannot be changed and cannot be revoked (vv. 8, 12, 15). By contrast, we know from Daniel 2:21 that Yhwh, the God of Daniel, can change anything:

He changes times and seasons,
deposes kings and sets up kings;
he gives wisdom to the wise
and knowledge to those who have understanding.
He reveals deep and hidden things;
he knows what is in the darkness,
and light dwells with him. (vv. 21-22)

There is something inherently revolutionary about this God!

As the narrative unfolds, Daniel obeys "the law of his God," and prays, "seeking mercy before his God," now a capital offense in Persia (v. 11). When the offense is reported to the king, the king agrees that his decree is binding and not changeable:

The thing stands fast, according to the laws of the Medes and Persians, which cannot be revoked. (v. 12)

• The conspirators convict Daniel:

> Daniel, one of the exiles from Judah, pays no atten-
> tion to you, O king, or to the interdict you have
> signed, but he is saying his prayers three times a
> day. (v. 13)

- The king is distressed, because his own edict has now
  come down lethally on his favorite Jew:

  > When the king heard the charge, he was very much
  > distressed. He was determined to save Daniel, and
  > until the sun went down he made every effort to res-
  > cue him. (v. 14)

- But the conspirators will not let Darius off his own
  hook. Not even the king can modify the rule:

  > Know, O King, that it is a law of the Medes and Per-
  > sians that no interdict or ordinance that the king
  > establishes can be changed. (v. 15)

- The sentence of the lions' den must be implemented,
  and a stone is used to secure the lions' den,

  > so that nothing might be changed concerning Dan-
  > iel. (v. 17)

The phrase has become a litany of certitude: "not change,
not change, not change." End of story, end of conspiracy, end
of Daniel's life. The absolute totalizing rule of empire has
reached its conclusion; Darius the lawmaker is helpless before
the conspirators. End of story.

Except at daybreak the next day even the king hopes for
something beyond his own decree. Even Darius half expects
that what cannot be changed will have been changed:

> Then, at break of day, the king got up and hurried to the
> den of lions. When he came near the den where Daniel was,
> he cried out anxiously to Daniel, "O Daniel, servant of the
> living God, has your God whom you faithfully serve been
> able to deliver you from the lions?" (vv. 19-20)

Darius hopes for "the living God," "your God." And he is not
disappointed! Daniel responds doxologically:

My God has sent his angel and shut the lions' mouths so
that they would not hurt me, because I was found blameless
before him; and also before you, O king, I have done no
wrong. (v. 22)

And Darius is "exceedingly glad" that his edict was overrid-
den. He is not angry about the inadequacy of his own decree.
Darius also ends doxologically:

> I make a decree, that in all my royal dominion people should
> tremble and fear before the God of Daniel:
> For he is the living God,
> enduring forever.
> His kingdom shall never be destroyed,
> and his dominion has no end.
> He delivers and rescues,
> he works signs and wonders in heaven and on earth;
> for he has saved Daniel
> from the power of the lions. (vv. 26-27)

The narrative evidences no hint of irony about the defeat that
Darius (who continues making decrees) faces as his own decree
is made penultimate and ineffective before the God who can
change all things, the one who deposes kings and sets up kings.

The issue is joined concerning the rule of the God of Israel
and the changeless decrees of the Medes and the Persians. In
the Old Testament, we meet this same unchanging law only
two other times. In Ezra 6, Darius decrees provisions for the
rebuilding of the temple in Jerusalem, and he declares:

> Furthermore I decree that if anyone alters this edict, a
> beam shall be pulled out of the house of the perpetrator,
> who then shall be impaled on it. The house shall be made a
> dunghill. May the God who has established his name there
> overthrow any king or people that shall put forth a hand
> to alter this, or to destroy this house of God in Jerusalem.
> I, Darius, make a decree; let it be done with all diligence.
> (vv. 11-12)

In Esther 1:19, Vashti is banished by the same intransigence of
the law of the Medes and the Persians.

In each narrative it is an absolute decree, offered by a totalizing regime that imagines it can administer all reality without dissent or variation or modification. These are the first instances with explicit reference to "the law of the Medes and the Persians." It is, however, not the first time Israel has met an absolute law offered by a totalizing regime. This is indeed the story of Pharaoh in the book of Exodus. Long before Darius, Pharaoh is a totalizer who allows nothing outside his domain, offering his absolute law:

> Get to your labors . . .
> Make [more] bricks . . .
> Go and get straw yourselves. . .
> Go now and work . . .
> You shall not lessen your daily number of bricks. (Exod 5:4, 7, 11, 18, 19)

The unchanging, absolutizing law is always about conduct that enhances the regime. We have no details, but clearly the Babylonians exercised that same totalizing propensity:

> I shall be mistress forever . . .
> I am, and there is no one besides me;
> I shall not sit as a widow or know the loss of children . . .
> No one sees me . . .
> I am, and there is no one besides me. (Isa 47:7, 8, 10)

And the ultimate indictment of Babylon by Yhwh:

> I was angry with my people,
> I profaned my heritage;
> I gave them into your hand,
> you showed them no mercy;
> on the aged you made your yoke exceedingly heavy. (47:6)

There can be no mercy for a regime that performs an unchanging law.

Every totalizing regime emits law that is absolute. The story of the Old Testament is of Jewish fidelity in the face of such law. And indeed, we ourselves know the same form of totalizing regimes, the totalizing of "law and order" ideology that imprisons everyone it can with its "Stand Your Ground" anxiety, the totalizing of a church that imagines unbounded authority specializing in wounding the noncompliant, the totalizing laws of race, class, and gender that are absolute and unaccommodating, unchanging and without mercy. It is an old story that runs from the Medes and Persians into our own contemporaneity.

II.

The burden of what I have to say about law in the Old Testament is that there is an alternative to the unchanging laws of the Medes and Persians, because the Torah of Yhwh is nestled in the zone of fidelity marked by *mispat* and *sedeqah, hesed* and *'emeth* and *raham*. Torah is rooted in the grace of transformation (that is, Sinai in the wake of Exodus) and is enacted as neighborly justice as an insistent alternative to Pharaoh's predatory regime. I am required to acknowledge, however, that there are dimensions of totalizing absolutism in Yhwh's Torah in the Old Testament. There are commandments that reflect primitive, patriarchal, exclusionary assumptions and practices and that sanction modes of brutalizing violence. Thus, concerning exclusionary practices, in addition to the purity codes, there is this:

> No one whose testicles are crushed or whose penis is cut off shall be admitted to the assembly of the Lord.
>
> Those born of an illicit union shall not be admitted to the assembly of the Lord . . .
>
> No Ammonite or Moabite shall be admitted to the assembly of the Lord. Even to the tenth generation none of their descendants shall be admitted to the assembly of the Lord. (Deut 23:1-3)

There are commandments for harsh punitive sanctions that reflect patriarchal totalizing:

If someone has a stubborn and rebellious son who will not obey his father and mother, who does not heed them when they discipline him, then his father and his mother shall take hold of him and bring him out to the elders of his town at the gate of that place. They shall say to the elders of his town, "This son of ours is stubborn and rebellious. He will not obey us. He is a glutton and a drunkard." Then all the men of the town shall stone him to death. So you shall purge the evil from your midst; and all Israel will hear, and be afraid. (Deut 21:18-21)

There are warrants for unrestrained violence toward enemies in the practice of *herem* as the ultimate mode of warfare:

But as for the towns of these peoples that the Lord our God is giving you as an inheritance, you must not let anything that breathes remain alive. You shall annihilate [with an infinitive absolute] them—the Hittites and the Amorites, the Canaanites and the Perizzites, the Hivites and the Jebusites—just as the Lord your God has commanded so that they may not teach you to do all the abhorrent things that they do for their gods, and you thus sin against the Lord your God. (Deut 20:16-18)

There is provision for treating slaves as property:

When a slave owner strikes a male or female slave with a rod and the slave dies immediately, the owner shall be punished. But if the slave survives a day or two, there is no punishment; for the slave is the owner's property ["silver"]. (Exod 21:20-21)

As you know, these examples are easy to spot and to multiply.

As you know further, interpreters have worked very hard to mitigate the harshness of these commandments, or to explain them away. It is easy enough to judge that these sorts of commandments are reflective of a cultural propensity in a violent and patriarchal society in which respect for the other was not much in purview. And of course every authorizing community tends to promote its interest and bias as fully authoritative and beyond criticism.

Given all of that, however, I judge that none of this explanatory reasoning is an adequate excuse for allowing Yhwh, the giver of these commandments, a pass for such provisions. I think, rather, that we must recognize that Yhwh, in Yhwh's own life, has a totalizing propensity that extends from the desire for unshared glory (see Isa 42:8; 48:11) to intense social control.[1] In that regard, Yhwh is too much like Pharaoh and Nebuchadnezzar and Darius, all of whom imagined their edicts to be unchangeable. Thus in Yhwh's own life and utterance, even allowing for all of the critical complexity we can muster, sometimes Yhwh's totalizing temptation overrides Yhwh's capacity for generously hosting the other. I suspect that is true even in the trajectory of the magisterial utterance that begins in Exodus 34:6-7 that juxtaposes the vocabulary of fidelity with the punishment to the third and fourth generations.[2] Thus Yhwh, in giving law, has a history of barbarism. In my judgment, Yhwh must be called to account for that, because that remembered history of divine barbarism continues to haunt synagogue and church, and too often provides warrant for continuing "morally grounded" barbarism. In that regard, Yhwh continues on in the world of "common theology" of the Near East, with its heavy accent on punitive sanctions.

III.

It is of course clear that there is another trajectory of Yhwh's commandments, or we would not be here. In deep tension with that totalizing temptation, there is a trajectory of commandments that rushes *toward the other* in generosity and hospitality performed as restorative justice. More than that, it is clear enough that this trajectory of reach toward the other comes to dominate the biblical tradition and is the wave of the future. This alternative trajectory of commandments has often been understood in terms of the "evolution of religion" toward "ethical monotheism." If, however, we are to be theologically serious and not satisfied with "history of religion," then we must entertain and struggle with the disclosure of God's own life that is a contested move away from the common theology of sanctions, to fidelity that is generative. It is argued, persuasively I think, that in our society the anxiety evoked around 9/11 has moved us toward an even greater propensity for punishment—witness "The New Jim Crow" and "Stand Your Ground."[3] Perhaps anxiety in Yhwh's life evoked laws of exclusionary harshness.

The biblical text, I would contend, is a movement in the counter direction: the presence of the other as a legitimate and eventually respected presence attests to an alternative to a totalizing compulsion. It is that propensity that is the future of law in the Old Testament, and the one I will consider here. I will propose that it is this dramatic embrace of the other in fidelity, slowly done to be sure, that is exactly an alternative to the immutability of the Medes and the Persians; it is changeability in the commandments, always done in contested ways, that permits the commandments to function as an effective generative force in the tradition, in the book, and among the people.

When we consider what set this alternative trajectory in motion, I suggest it is Yhwh's participation in the Exodus narrative that positions Yhwh as lawgiver in a new way. The Exodus narrative and its dramatic performance of emancipation is a way in which Yhwh was summoned, by the cries of the slaves, to participate in the drama of emancipation and in conflict with the totalism of Pharaoh. It is no doubt true that law arises from narrative, as Robert Cover has so persuasively insisted.[4] The narrative of the Exodus is the venue for a generative view of law in the Old Testament, a venue in which both Israel and Yhwh participate. As a result, when Israel arrived at Sinai in Exodus 19, the scars, tambourines, and witness of the Exodus were still palpable in Israel. They were, more than that, palpable to Yhwh as well. Who would have thought that

Yhwh would be so drawn into the narrative struggle that Yhwh would come to the recognition of Israel as "my firstborn son" (Exod 4:22)? This is indeed solidarity with what Terry Eagleton has called "the scum of earth."[5] It is that narrative drama that changed Yhwh and that made Yhwh changeable, because here was a chance to observe firsthand the immutability of Pharaoh that was a harbinger of the Medes and the Persians. The Exodus was a disruption of the immutable. As a result, I propose, the discourse at Sinai, and the continuing tradition from Sinai in interpretation, can only be understood in the wake of that narrative alert.

The tradition of law in the Old Testament begins at Sinai when Israel arrives in Exodus 19. The initial interaction at Sinai is quite remarkable.[6] Yhwh speaks first, as though to claim dominance for the meeting. Yhwh recalls the Exodus:

> You have seen what I did to the Egyptians, and how I bore
> you on eagles' wings and brought you to myself. (v. 4)

Israel is witness; Yhwh is agent. The destination of the long journey from Egypt was not Sinai. It is "brought you *to me*." It is about a relationship. And then Yhwh shifts from memory to present moment, a statement that begins with a huge condition:

> If you obey my voice and keep my covenant, you shall be my
> treasured possession out of all the peoples. (v. 5)

The relationship on offer is conditional. The condition is not production, not more bricks. It is the primal commitment of loyalty expressed in two ways. First, "if you listen" ("obey" is a usual but weak translation). The imperative of *shema'* is relational. You are addressed, and you must answer; you must attend to what is being said. The imperative is with an infinitive absolute, "really listen," willing to pay close attention. The imperative is matched by "keep my covenant." There had been reference to covenant in Exodus 2:25 and 6:4-5; but those are allusions back to Abraham in Genesis. There had been nothing of a covenant with this "mixed multitude" (Exod 12:38). It was likely a surprise to the newly emancipated slaves that the emancipator intended a continuing relationship with them.

The prospect from such intense *listening and keeping* comes in a huge "then" that matches the "if." Then, only then, this "mixed multitude" will be "my treasured possession." No such "if" had been spoken to Abraham. But no such declared intimacy as "treasured possession" had been offered to Abraham either. This is a most generous offer; but it entails performed loyalty. It consists in the reality of a relationship; it is not performance of a rule. The rules that are to follow, and the interpretation of the rules that are to follow the rules, are all exegesis. They are not the substance. The substance is "listening and keeping," listening that will define the future. That listening, in the long interpretive tradition, required the listening in this passionate relationship to be actualized in concrete acts. Don't talk of listening; show me! We have known, even before Luther, that the concrete performance of a relationship, when it is emptied of personal loyalty and reduced to a set of rules, is already a failed relationship.

But not here! Here there is readiness and eagerness. In verse 8, before any commandments are given, the emancipated slaves sign on with eager loyalty:

Everything that the Lord has spoken we will do.

No hesitation, no reluctance, no request for specificity. It appears to me that this pre-commandment assent to commandments is motivated by the assumption that whatever concrete conditions the emancipatory God articulates, they will be much preferable to the conditions of Pharaoh. They have reason to think this, as Yhwh had nullified the commandments of Pharaoh that were until then unchangeable. It is possible, I think, to sort out the ten commandments of Pharaoh in Exodus 5. They are all variations on the one insistent commandment of Pharaoh: "Make more bricks." And now

Israel understands that whatever else it might concern, Yhwh's alternative conditionality will concern not a brick quota but rather the great covenantal possibilities of fidelity . . . *mispat, sedeqah, hesed, amunah, raham*. Thus, the commandments that are to follow are alternative commandments, counter to Pharaoh.[7] The drama of Sinai is to complete the rejection of Pharaoh's demands and to embrace Yhwh's expectation of loyalty. The drama of Sinai is to delineate perspective, policy, and practice—habits if you will—that will sustain and solidify the emancipation of the Exodus. Exodus was a movement, an irresistible movement of emancipation. And now Sinai is the hard work of transposing a *movement* into something like an *institutional regime* that in principle is dead set against totalism. Here is law that aims to preclude totalism and authorize alternative. Upon receipt of the Israelite response via Moses, Yhwh responds to Moses:

> I am going to come down to you in a dense cloud, in order that the people may hear when I speak with you and so trust you ever after. (v. 9)

It is as though to say, "This is what I have been waiting for! I am coming to you." This is like Eisenhower going to Korea, the entry of the new sovereign with new proposals to a newly loyal, emancipated people. The purpose of Yhwh's visit, we are told, is to make Moses a human voice of divine utterance, (a) that Israel may hear (*shema'*) and (b) that the people may trust Moses forever. Provision is already made for a human voice that will transmit divine utterance. Everything then will be about hearing and trusting. This does not sound like immutability. This sounds more like a continuing conversation. Soon enough Israel will speak in response—but not yet. Now it is divine utterance and Israel listening.

The stage is set for the divine disclosure that will assume the continuing force and social possibility of the Exodus. This divine disclosure is artistically framed. Preceding the divine utterance is the staging of a theophany with the necessary pageantry of smoke, fire, trumpets, thunder, lightning, and the violent shaking of the mountain (Exod 19:16-25). This is none other than the new sovereign who does not arrive, as Pharaoh, with a procession of chariots. This is the creator, attended by the massive force of creation. Following the divine utterance is a response of fear and the recognition of Moses as human mediator (20:18-21), a provision already signaled in 19:9. The utterance is very special and distinctive, framed between *theophany* and *mediation*: non-negotiable utterances, ten of them!

IV.

So what might be said freshly about the Big Ten? I propose only this: they are counter commands to the commands of Pharaoh. They are counter commands to the immutability of the Medes and Persians. They are counter commands to every effort at totalizing, including the totalism of anti-neighborly economics in our own time, and totalizing orthodoxies that know too much of wounding truth. The words are familiar to us, but the context via Pharaoh and Exodus requires a different reading of these inherently subversive commandments.

The three commandments that attest the governance of Yhwh propose an alternative to the absolutism of Pharaoh. The rhetoric of the commandments bespeaks a kind of entitlement for Yhwh about which Martin Noth could write:

> The vital element in the content of the Old Testament laws must be what is peculiar to them alone. . . . It appears to me that we can grasp that peculiar factor under one consistent viewpoint: they are provisions which seek to ensure the exclusive nature of the relationship between God and people, between Yahweh and the Israelite tribes, or (in other words) which guard against a defection in any form from the sole God, who is thought of as a partner to the covenant. The history of religions by and large knows nothing of this concept of "defection," because it is solely a consequence of a strict requirement of restriction to a single God.[8]

But we mistake this claim of exclusiveness if we read the commandments without the claim's narrative context—namely, deliverance "out of the land of Egypt, out of the house of bondage." This is singular loyalty to the emancipator. Yhwh's first commandment is exactly the kind of utterance we might expect from Pharaoh. But they are, in fact, in contrast: Pharaoh was a totalizer; Yhwh is the sponsor of what Emmanuel Levinas terms "infinity" in his exposition of "totality and infinity."[9] In his purview, infinity is the urge that everything is possible because nothing is an unchangeable given. Everything is possible with the emancipator, because his life is outside the domain of the system of enslavement.

Divine exclusion comes with two additional provisions: first, no graven images, no commoditization, no visible icon to situate loyalty in anything but a relationship of trust that is not controlled. Second, no mobilization of the divine name or divine identity or divine will for other projects, because the other projects (nation-state, war, church, stewardship campaign, Pharaoh's enslavement system, whatever) will siphon off the edgy possibility of the relationship. Yhwh comes with no hyphen, no usage that will predictably end in brick quotas. Pharaoh could not appear in public without his entourage of extravagant visual imagery:

> Removing his signet ring from his hand, Pharaoh put it on Joseph's hand; he arrayed him in garments of fine linen, and put a gold chain around his neck. He had him ride in the chariot of his second-in-command, and they cried out in front of him, "Bow the knee!" (Gen 41:42-43)

Pharaoh was inconceivable without his brick quotas, his exhibit of wealth, his storehouses of monopoly, and his work force of cheap labor that made it all possible. The history of idolatry in the biblical communities is the endless, restless effort to hyphenate the God of Sinai to images or causes or programs. But Yhwh is so unlike all of the idols. As the psalmist understood so well, the hyphenated gods become objects of worship that need to be carried and are without power:

> Their idols are silver and gold,
> the work of human hands.
> They have mouths, but do not speak;
> eyes, but do not see.
> They have ears, but do not hear;
> noses, but do not smell.
> They have hands, but do not feel;
> feet, but do not walk.
> They make no sound in their throats. (Ps 115:4-7; see Isa 46:1-2)

The last six of the Big Ten—parents, murder, adultery, stealing, false witness, coveting—imagine an alternative to the brickyard. In the brickyard, with its coercive order and its intrinsic violence, it is not likely that there could be trust, because all compete for the same scarce resources. I have only lately noticed that the terse tenth commandment sounds the word "neighbor" three times:

> You shall not covet your *neighbor's* house; you shall not covet your *neighbor's* wife, or male or female slave, or ox, or donkey, or anything that belongs to your *neighbor*. (Exod 20:17)

These divine expectations and summons are about generative and sustainable neighborliness. We need not romanticize "neighbor" as one with whom we share intimacy. Rather, the term refers to members who share a common destiny and so are ordered according to a common good, a commonality that requires that their relationship be other than that of rivals, competitors, or threats.

Surely in Pharaoh's Egypt there were no neighbors. In his exposition of Chilean society under Pinochet, William Cavanaugh describes a state of quiet terror in which surveillance so permeated every dimension of society that no one could trust anyone, and the possibility of a common good was precluded.[10] It is difference in degree, not in kind, in our society of predatory competition propelled by anxiety and sustained by cheap labor. No neighborly trust is possible, no passion for the common good; any summons to the good of the neighbor is an intrusion in the predatory economy.

Where there is no neighborhood and no neighbors, as there was not in Egypt,

> there can be murder, because the others are all dispensable;
>
> there can be adultery, because all the others have been commoditized for sale or for use;
>
> there can be theft, even wage theft, because the money always belongs to those who have the capacity to take it;
>
> there can be false witness, because who's to say?
>
> there can be coveting, rapacious greed, in which the big ones eat the little ones.

Eventually, the erosion of human possibility will reach the family, in which unproductive parents are expendable. The outcome is predictable when the gods of Pharaoh are mobilized and everyone becomes tradable.

And then, in the midst of such predation, comes this awesome utterance, "neighbor, neighbor, neighbor," in which the ones next to us with whom we live are redefined and cast in other roles, because the emancipatory God is a neighborhood-sponsoring agent. The Exodus was a journey from *the scarcity of slavery* to *the abundance of neighborly bread*, a prospect impossible in Egypt but possible in the wilderness, where

> some gather[ed] more, some less. . . . Those who gathered little had no shortage; they gathered as much as each of them needed. (Exod 16:17-18)

Patrick Miller, in an incisive article, has exposited the "sabbatic principle" of sabbath, Year of Release, Jubilee Year, all of a piece.[11] He has suggested, moreover, that the fourth commandment on sabbath is the lynchpin of the Big Ten because it looks back to the rest of God in creation, and it looks forward to the restfulness of the neighborhood, for in a genuine neighborhood there is no cause for predatory anxiety. Sabbath is an occasion for the "peace of God" that has no production schedule: (a) this God in peaceableness wants or needs nothing; (b) neighborliness in peaceableness means a deep relaxation from fear, anxiety, and the need to produce. The "as you" in the Deuteronomy version of the sabbath commandment is a mighty protest against social stratification based on economic difference (Deut 5:14). For sure, there could be no sabbath in Egypt, not for the slaves, not for the taskmasters, not for the supervisors, not even for Pharaoh, because the ideology of scarcity allows no rest, never to imagine, never to play, never to worship, never to pause in the anxiety that remains definitional.

The Torah is a witness to God-authorized possibility. And Israel is to listen. Israel is to listen in the infinitive absolute. And so Israel answers in Exodus 24:

All the words that the Lord has spoken we will do. (v. 3)

All that the Lord has spoken we will do, and we will be obedient. (v. 7)

This is a pledge to attend to the counterworld of Yhwh so as to resist the coercive world of Pharaoh. The entire transaction concerns a continued and continuing exodus and an oft-performed exit from the world of Pharaoh, because Pharaoh has the immense capacity to draw back into the predator world of scarcity that converts every would-be neighbor into a commodity. It is long noticed that in the second vow of loyalty in verse 7, Israel promises, "We will do and we will hear" (NRSV has "be obedient"). We might have expected hearing before doing. But the terms overlap. Hearing is not done with one's ears alone. Hearing is done with one's entire being. Listening is practical engaged attentiveness that consists in a bodily act of loyalty to the world on offer from Yhwh. Thus, the Big Ten articulate an immense either/or that continues to haunt the community of Israel:

> See, I have set before you today life and prosperity, death and adversity. (Deut 30:15)

> If the Lord is God, follow him; but if Baal, then follow him. (1 Kgs 18:21)

> Enter through the narrow gate; for the gate is wide and the road is easy that leads to destruction. (Matt 7:13)

V.

We have a hint of a human mediator in Exodus 19:9 and a con-firmation of it in 20:19 when the people, in their frightened response to the utterance of Yhwh, address Moses:

> You speak to us, and we will listen; but do not let God speak to us or we will die.

The provision for a mediator indicates that there is more to come from Yhwh after the Big Ten. And because there is more to come, Israel must continue to listen. Israel will con-tinue to be addressed by the Lord of the commandments. And the reason more will be given and Israel must continue to lis-ten is that the Torah of Yhwh is not fixed, closed, or settled. Unlike the law of the Medes and Persians, the Torah of Yhwh is open, ready, and able to move into always new territory. In Israel's tradition and on into Judaism, that mode of new utter-ance is in the practice of interpretation. It is this act of inter-pretation that assures the dynamism of the Torah, that makes it possible that the Ten Commandments, seemingly uttered in a way that gives closure, are endlessly open to future interpre-tation that consists in contested negotiation about what they mean and require in any particular circumstance.[12] We know, speaking critically, that the large corpus of Torah in the Old Testament consists in the appropriation and incorporation of large bodies of texts from a variety of circumstances.[13] In con-text, however, that appropriation and incorporation are acts of interpretation that extended or altered the requirements. Thus, the Torah consists not in a set of rules but in fact in an ongoing conversation that takes into account new times, new circumstances, and newly awakened social sensibility.

We may consider three trajectories of tradition by which the initial utterances of Sinai are given fresh and greater force.

1. At Sinai, Yhwh is disclosed as a forceful sovereign God before whom Israel is frightened. We do not yet get at Sinai the great vocabulary of fidelity that I have previously delineated. Any totalizing by Yhwh is broken open in the narrative immediately following that of Sinai—namely, the narrative of the golden calf. Yhwh's initial response to the affront of the calf is appropriate to a totalizing master:

> Now let me alone, so that my wrath may burn hot against them, and I may consume them; and of you I will make a great nation. (Exod 32:10)

Yhwh's rage, however, is mitigated by the insistence of Moses, who talks Yhwh into a change of mind (see vv. 11-14). This God is capable of altered response, not as one who gives dictums from on high, but as a partner who is deeply situated in a bilateral relationship. The mitigation of the initial divine rage goes further in the interaction of chapter 33, in which Moses refuses to back down before Yhwh or give in to Yhwh. In response to Moses' insistence, Yhwh declares his capacity for grace and mercy that had not heretofore been disclosed at Sinai:

> I will make my goodness pass before you, and I will proclaim before you the name, "The Lord"; and I will be gracious to whom I will be gracious, and I will show mercy on whom I will show mercy. (33:19)

This is a sovereign who retains freedom of action, but it is a form of freedom beyond the rigor of rage. "Grace and mercy" were not a part of the initial Sinai disclosure, but Yhwh has been pressed there by circumstance. Moreover, in the faceoff of chapter 34, Yhwh eventually, in the wake of alienation, for the first time calls out the great vocabulary of fidelity:

The Lord, the Lord,
a God merciful and gracious, slow to anger,
and abounding in steadfast love and faithfulness,
keeping steadfast love for the thousandth generation,
forgiving iniquity and transgression and sin. (34:6-7)

Then follows the demanding sovereignty of Yhwh (v. 7), a petition by Moses (v. 9), and a readiness of Yhwh to reengage covenant (v. 10). In the process of articulating 33:19 and 34:6-7, Israel learns more about the character and inclination of Yhwh than was known at Sinai. It is the brokenness of the relationship that evokes Yhwh to such self-disclosure. It is, moreover, that same brokenness writ large in the tradition that continues to disclose the changeability of Yhwh in response to circumstance. Thus, it is in the eighth-century crisis that Hosea is led to voice the pathos of Yhwh (Hos 11:8-9). It is the sixth-century crisis that generates, as I have shown, the vocabulary of fidelity for Yhwh that was not available earlier. The listening of Israel made available the richness and depth of the character of Yhwh as an agent of grace and mercy and as a performer of justice.

2. We have seen that the Decalogue is a vision, a summons, and a vocation concerning neighborliness, a sharp contrast to the anti-neighborliness of Pharaoh. Of course the question lingers over the entire tradition concerning the identity of the neighbor whom we are mandated to love. At present, the contested catalogue of neighbors includes gays, immigrants, and Muslims. But such contestation is always the case. As Israel continues to listen, the "neighbor" highlighted in the tenth commandment is fleshed out:

- It turns out, belatedly, that the neighbor is "the one who shows mercy" (Luke 10:37).
- But of course long before that parable, the inventory of those to be loved in covenant is variously extended. Already, in Exodus 22, it must stun those who would love neighbor to hear a larger mandate. Yhwh abruptly

becomes the enforcer who protects resident aliens, widows, and orphans:

> You shall not wrong or oppress a resident alien, for you were aliens in the land of Egypt. You shall not abuse any widow or orphan. If you do abuse them, when they cry out to me, I will surely heed their cry. (22:21-23)

The reference to "heed their cry" is a clear allusion back to the Exodus cry that God heard. Now the circle of neighborliness is wider . . . widow, orphan, immigrant (variously translated as "stranger" or "alien").

• And in the very next verse, the circle of engagement extends even to the poor:

> If you lend money to my people, to the poor among you, you shall not deal with them as a creditor; you shall not exact interest from them. If you take your neighbor's cloak in pawn, you shall restore it before the sun goes down; for it may be your neighbor's only clothing to use as cover; in what else shall that person sleep? And if your neighbor cries out to me, I will listen, for I am compassionate. (vv. 25-27)

Moses already knows about loan sharks and excessive collateral, and the response of this God who is compassionate.

If Israel had not kept listening, it might have thought that "neighbor" meant only likeminded male shareholders in the landowning company of Israel. Further listening, however, extended the command beyond "neighbor's" house, "neighbor's" wife, anything that is your "neighbor's" to widows' houses, to immigrants' wives, to anything that belongs to the poor, the orphan, or the widow. As Israel listens, the depth and urgency of the old commandments become more acute and more demanding. It will await that belated rabbi to finally extend the circle to "your enemy":

Love your enemies and pray for those who persecute
you. . . . If you greet only your brothers and sisters, what
more are you doing than others? Do not even the Gentiles
do the same? Be perfect, therefore, as your heavenly Father
is perfect. (Matt 5:44, 47-48)

But the tradition is already underway. The move from *neighbor* to *stranger* (*widow, orphan, immigrant, poor*) is on the way to
enemy. The categories change, because this fluid, lively God
keeps altering the terms of the interaction of covenant as circumstance requires. These are not set rules but personal commitments that are kept under review and pushed relentlessly
in new directions.

3. To "keep listening" means that the God tempted to
totalism turns to the vocabulary of *fidelity*. To "keep listening"
means that the circle of neighborliness becomes more radical
and more inclusive. And now we can see, given the emergence
of the compassion of God in the interpretive process and the
expansiveness of neighborliness is that interpretive process,
that "keep listening" also extends the rule of sabbath that is
the lynchpin of the Decalogue. It is already in the Decalogue
a defiance against Pharaoh, against life defined by commodity and its accumulation. Now, in the Year of Release (Deut
15:1-18), Moses shows that the sabbath is practice of neighborly
economics, a strategy for giving the poor a respite from debt.[14]
With the intensity of five absolute infinitives, with warning
against Pharaonic reactions that are "tightfisted" and "hard-
hearted," and with a poignant recall of the Exodus, the commandment now subordinates the sphere of economics to the
requirements of neighborliness. Moses is determined that
in the covenantal neighborhood there can be no permanent
underclass, that conviction requires cancellation of debts,
the curbing of economic predation, and the full economic
participation and well-being of those who have been lost in
the economic shuffle. As Israel keeps listening, it reaches to
the Jubilee Year, the amazing capstone of covenantal ethics

in which property is subordinated to an emancipatory vision of society. Midway in his exposition of the Jubilee, Moses declares, in speaking of the "impoverished,"

> For they are my servants whom I brought out of the land of Egypt; they shall not be sold as slaves are sold. You shall not rule over them with harshness, but shall fear your God. (Lev 25:42-43)

The grounding is the rescue from Egypt. They are not sold as slaves because they belong to the emancipatory God. They are not sold as slaves to the predatory economy that pursues them. At the end of his discourse, Moses will declare:

> For to me the people of Israel are servants; they are my servants whom I brought out from the land of Egypt: I am the Lord your God (v. 55).

They belong to me, says God, and not to Pharaoh.

Imagine that if Israel had thought Yhwh was finished speaking at Sinai, Israel would have ceased to listen, because it had already heard everything.

- If Israel had not listened longer, it would not have known that the absolutizing God of Sinai is, via the narrative of the Golden Calf, a God of *hesed*, *amunah*, and *raham*.
- If Israel had not listened longer, it would have limited the sphere of the neighbor of the tenth commandment and not included *widows*, *orphans*, *immigrants*, *the poor*, and eventually *enemies* whom are to be loved.
- If Israel had not listened longer, it would not have known that the requirement of work stoppage on Sabbath is in fact a refusal of Pharaoh's predatory economy.
- If Israel had accepted the declaration of the Medes and Persians, it might have frozen law into a safe set of formulations and kept thinking in terms of "original intent." If Israel had not listened further, it would have missed the point and failed in the ongoing requirements

of covenant. It belongs to God's people to keep listening, because this is the God who is "still speaking."

VI.

A propensity toward totalizing is voiced by Moses in
Deuteronomy:

> You must therefore be careful to do as the Lord your God
> has commanded you; shall not turn *to the right or to the
> left*. (5:32)

> [Concerning the judges] You must carry out fully the law
> that they interpret for you or the ruling that they announce
> to you; do not turn aside from the decision that they
> announce to you, either *to the right or to the left*. (17:11)

> [Concerning the king] . . . diligently observing all the words
> of this law and these statutes, neither exalting himself above
> other members of the community nor turning aside from
> the commandment, either *to the right or to the left*. (17:19-20;
> see 28:14)

The commandments, decisions, and interpretations are the
final statements that require absolute obedience. It turns out,
however, that this dictum of absoluteness has an openness to
it that we do not anticipate. That openness makes the book of
Deuteronomy the quintessential book of continued listening;
in the book of Deuteronomy, Moses continues to speak and
speak and speak beyond Sinai. It is the great script of interpretive dynamism. And Israel must listen continually, of course
beginning with the famous *shema*':

> Hear, O Israel: The Lord is our God, the Lord alone. (6:4)

But then also:

> *Hear* O Israel, the statutes and ordinances that I am
> addressing to you today; you shall learn them and observe
> them diligently. (5:1)

> *Hear*, O Israel! You are about to cross the Jordan today, to
> go in and dispossess nations larger and greater than you,
> great cities, fortified to the heavens. (9:1)

The blessing, if you *obey* (*hear*) the commandments of the Lord your God that I am commanding you today. (11:27)

Be careful to *obey* (*hear*) all these words that I command you today. (12:28)

The Lord your God you shall follow, him alone you shall fear, his commandments you shall keep, his voice you shall *obey* (*hear*), him you shall serve, and to him you shall hold fast. (13:4)

All the people will *hear* and be afraid, and will not act presumptuously again. (17:13)

Assemble the people—men, women, and children, as well as the aliens residing in your towns—so that they may *hear* and learn to fear the Lord your God and to observe diligently all the words of this law. (31:12)

This double aspect of (a) *fixity* without adding or subtracting or turning to the right or to the left on the one hand, and (b) *continuous speaking* and *continued listening* on the other hand gives the book of Deuteronomy an amazing quality of dialogic, dynamic power that is a model and exemplar of law in Israel. This is "settled law," always to be unsettled by more speaking and more listening.

As you know, the lynchpin of law in Deuteronomy is the Decalogue in Deuteronomy 5, quoted word for word from Sinai. Except that it is not! Spectacularly, when we get to the fourth commandment from Sinai on sabbath (5:12-15), we remember that sabbath is to be kept because the creator rested on day seven. But here, without notation, sabbath is to be kept because "you" remember being slaves in Egypt, delivered by Yhwh's outstretched hand, so that the Exodus is the deep work stoppage of all work stoppages. It is a good thing that Israel kept listening, elsewise Israel might have thought sabbath was simply to be in sync with creation and creator; but now, in this fresh listening, Israel knows that sabbath is the great socioeconomic equalizer, because "your" slave and "your" donkey and the immigrant will be "like you" on that day, ceasing for a day all social injustice and differentiation. Sabbath is, in new hearing, the font of an emancipatory hermeneutic.

Thus, we are put on notice right away at the Decalogue that God is still speaking and that Israel must be still listening, because there is more to hear. This modification of the commandment from which we should not "turn right or left" makes Deuteronomy an odd book, and an odd mode of law. When we ask about the book of Deuteronomy and its character and intention, we may notice three specific answers.

1. Deuteronomy is a *copy.* Thus, in Deuteronomy 17:18, the king is to keep a "copy" of "this Torah" at hand . . . *deuteros,* thus the name "Deuteronomy." But what if it is not a copy? What if it is a "second" version, a standard version, or a revised standard version, or a new revised standard version, or a new revised standard living version, or a new international Bible, or all of the above? Every reading (including this one) is a new account of Torah, and it will not do to imagine that these new readings are simply reiterations. They are replications changed to the right and to the left, by translation, by application, by interpretation, by shaping old laws in a dozen conversations.

2. Deuteronomy is *exegesis.* Already in 1:5, at the very outset, we are told "Moses undertook to expound this Torah." It is a tricky word, "expound." It signifies, in any case, that Moses did not simply reiterate. He added interpretation and explanation and application, as would Ezra after him:

> So they read from the book, from the law of God, with interpretation. They gave the sense, that the people understood the reading. (Neh 8:8)

And after Ezra, in the wake of Moses, came many expoundings by many rabbis and preachers and theologians, especially the Great Rabbi who said, "But I say unto you."

3. Third, Deuteronomy is an *act of making contemporary* (*Vergegenwaertigung*). So Moses introduces the Decalogue:

> Hear, O Israel, the statutes and ordinances that I am addressing to you today; you shall learn them and observe

them diligently. The Lord our God made a covenant with us at Horeb. Not with our ancestors did the Lord make this covenant, but with us, who are all of us here alive today. (5:1-3)

The rhetoric is intense: us . . . all of us . . . here . . . alive . . . today. The book of Deuteronomy transports Sinai law into the land of Canaan or, if we are to credit current criticism, into the Persian Empire, and so into many venues that require more than reiteration. The designation of a mediator at Sinai opens the way for many mediators, for interpretation, contention, and always fresh hearing. It turns out that the commandment-giver at Sinai did not remain at that old mountain but comes along with Israel on the way, in many new versions, in exegesis, in contemporaneity.

The corpus of laws in Deuteronomy 12–25 may indeed be a mishmash of many materials. However, S. A. Kaufman, Georg Braulik, and now John Walton have proposed that this corpus follows the outline of the Decalogue.[15] But now the Decalogue comes with huge expansive interpretations, so that the grace-grounded, justice-providing Torah of Yhwh always requires new hearing, and so new action, new practice, and new policy.

Thus, we may consider the easy case of the sabbath commandment that now authorizes work stoppage for slaves, immigrants, and donkeys. The hypothesis holds that the sabbath commandment is expanded into the commandments of Deuteronomy 14:22–16:17 and, most remarkably, the Year of Release (15:1-18). The parallel between Sinai and Deuteronomy is at many points inexact and requires a good bit of imagination to make it work. I was interested to see how the great commandments on civic justice in Deuteronomy were placed in the hypothesis. Walton subsumed the remarkable statutes of Deuteronomy 23–24 under "theft" and "false witness"; they might better be seen as an exposition of "covet." However that may be, it is clear that the exposition of Deuteronomy is preoccupied with neighborly justice that goes well beyond the terseness of Sinai for the sake of an agrarian economy under threat with the emergence of poverty. So Moses, still speaking, with Israel still listening, has it this way:

> You shall not charge interest on loans to another Israelite, interest on money, interest on provisions, interest on anything that is lent. (23:19)

> When you make your neighbor a loan of any kind, you shall not go into the house to take the pledge. You shall wait outside, while the person to whom you are making the loan brings the pledge out to you. If the person is poor, you shall not sleep in the garment given you as the pledge. You shall give the pledge back by sunset, so that your neighbor may sleep in the cloak and bless you. (24:10-13)

> You shall not withhold the wages of poor and needy laborers, whether other Israelites or aliens who reside in your land in one of your towns. (24:14)

> You shall not deprive a resident alien or an orphan of justice; you shall not take a widow's garment in pledge. (24:17)

> When you reap your harvest in your field and forget a sheaf in the field, you shall not go back to get it; it shall be left for the alien, the orphan, and the widow, so that the Lord your God may bless you in all your undertakings. When you beat your olive trees, do not strip what is left; it shall be left for the alien, the orphan, and the widow. When you gather the grapes of your vineyard, do not glean what is left; it shall be for the alien, the orphan, and the widow. Remember that you were a slave in the land of Egypt; therefore I am commanding you today to do this. (24:19-22)

These provisions are so remarkable that Frank Crüsemann could characterize them as "the first social safety net."[16] The final regulation identifies the three great money crops of that economy: grain, wine, and olive oil. It focuses on the three populations of the vulnerable: widows, orphans, and immigrants. It directs that these money crops should in part be deferred for the vulnerable, and all because of Exodus memory.

Where does Moses get this daring view of a neighborly economy? Not from Sinai! Perhaps from the Exodus narrative. More likely God is still speaking, still exegeting, still pressing Torah to contemporaneity, still redefining reality in terms of the neighborhood, still insisting that the God who *reaches in grace* and *restores in justice* will order creation differently. This is inspired stuff! It is imagined stuff! It is emergent law propelled by *vision* rooted in *narrative*.

Not surprisingly, there was clearly pushback from the totalizers. There is, for example, an inventory in Deuteronomy 14:1-21 for purity that will separate and excludes. Deuteronomy can be busy "purging the evil that is in your midst," concerning anything that disrupts established order (13:6; 17:2, 12; 19:13, 19; 21:21). This pushback authorized brutality in war and in the harsh maintenance of civic order. The footprint of totalizing is all over Deuteronomy. To the contrary, however, anticipatory exposition is on the way, and we are left with listening work to do. Near the end of the corpus, Moses limits public punishment to forty lashes so that "your neighbor" will not be "degraded" (25:1-3). Degraded—that is, belittled! Who would have expected that the great God of heavy sanctions would pause to curb humiliation? "Forty lashes" is not a daring limit. But it is there, even if still a long way from forgiving seventy times seven! But it is there, for continued listening.

Thus, the book of Deuteronomy knows the law to be a continuing conversation. It is about "scattering" in exile of a community that will not listen, a warning and a sanction. But it is also a "gathering" of a community that Yhwh wills to sustain, and a summons that issues in forgiveness, generosity, and restoration (30:3-5). Children of the Torah, including us, will continue to negotiate, expound, exegete, and contemporize, moving between warning and assurance, between sanction and restoration, between scattering and gathering, glimpsing in the process divine grace that reaches beyond and divine justice that restores.

VII.

It is a ready move from the conversation about law in Deuteronomy to the conversation about law in the book of Psalms. Patrick Miller has described the way in which the "motivational rhetoric" of the two are parallel, and he has explored the "Torah piety" that is voiced and advocated in Psalms 1, 19, and 119.[17] These psalms, moreover, are strategically placed to aid in the reading of the entire Psalter from the perspective of Torah. Thus, we may judge that the Psalter, given its canonical shape, is a meditation on the law, a Torah exactly celebrated in the introduction of Psalm 1:

> Happy are those who do not follow the advice of the wicked,
> or take the path that sinners tread,
> or sit in the seat of scoffers;
> but their delight is in the law of the Lord,
> and on his law they meditate day and night. (vv. 1-2)

The psalm proposes, as does the tradition of Deuteronomy, that obedience to the Torah issues in prosperity and well-being, thus providing a quite pragmatic motivation for obedient hearing. Taken in this way, it possible to understand obedience to Torah as a "work," as Luther surely did. When such practical considerations dominate, the process of obedient hearing is emptied of dialogic, relational dynamic and is reduced to a calculation.

But of course such a pragmatic calculation is a distortion of the glad listening obedience that the traditions of Deuteronomy and Psalms have in mind. In Psalm 119 there is a deep love of and passion for the Torah that is a sum of joy. But obedience to Torah is not to "earn" a good future. Thus, the psalm readily petitions God for life and does not claim life via obedience:

> Deal bountifully with your servant,
> so that I may live and observe your word . . . (v. 17)
> My soul clings to the dust;

revive me according to your word . . . (v. 25)
Turn my eyes from looking at vanities;
give me life in your ways . . . (v. 37)
See, I have longed for your precepts;
in your righteousness give me life . . . (v. 40)
This is my comfort in my distress,
that your promise gives me life . . . (v. 50)
In your steadfast love spare my life,
so that I may keep the decrees of your mouth . . . (v. 88)
Uphold me according to your promise, that I may live. (v. 116;
    see vv. 149, 156, 159)

Life is a gift of God; for that reason urgent appeal is made to God that God should continue in fidelity to give that life upon which the speaker is dependent.

In context, obedience to Torah is not a rule for rewards. In Israel, hearing obedience is a concrete, practical, bodily, quotidian performance of human fidelity before God. It is not a cause of fidelity; it is not a consequence of fidelity. It is itself the enactment of fidelity. It is the joy of being in sync with the Lord of covenant, the sense of companionship in doing the things in which the partner delights. The delight in such obedience is not in its outcome but in its performance, because it is a gift to come down where you ought to be—namely, in sync with and in the presence of God.

Such a performance can of course become phony in the sense of Winnicott's "false self," and surely Job's friends represent that seduction.[18] But such a distortion does not define the act of hearing, because obedience to Torah is not a work but a habit, a habit of the heart that becomes a way of life.

One clear example of such a "habit" of obedience is offered in the book *Lest Innocent Blood Be Shed*, a narrative about the way in which the French Huguenot village of Le Chambon took risks to hide Jews during the war.[19] They did so under the shrewd leadership of their pastor. Later on, when a son of one of the Jewish survivors of the village went to engage the villagers about their risky action, they simply shrugged their shoulders as if to say, "That is who we are; that is what we do." For all the risk, it was basically a deep, almost unreflective decision to live out one's faith in obedience.

In his earlier narrative concerning Jews in the Soviet Union, Elie Wiesel reports on being in Moscow on the occasion of the Jewish Festival of the Joy of Torah, Simchat Torah. He observed a Jewish woman who lived in fear as a Jew. But at the festival day, she boldly danced in the street with the Kremlin only ten minutes away. She told Wiesel:

> "What does it matter what they think of us . . . it's what we think that counts. . . . I'll tell you why I am a Jew. Because I like to sing."[20]

Wiesel concludes:

> They danced until midnight without rest, to let the city know that they were Jews.[21]

She danced the Torah! Such obedience is not a means to an end. It is an end, an end of joy, well-being, companionship, and the ongoing task of interpretation. For the sake of such joy beyond calculation, the psalmist is able to say:

> I hate the double-minded,
> but I love your law . . .
> I long for your salvation, O Lord,
> and your law is my delight.
> Let me live that I may praise you,
> and let your ordinances help me. (119:113, 174-75)

VIII.

I have taken "law" to refer to law in the Old Testament, my field of competence. Obviously the question of law is greater and more complex in public life than it is in the Old Testament. I would imagine, however, that the key issues I have traced in the Old Testament are the same issues in dispute in larger public conversation—namely, the *non-negotiability* of the law and *the continuing process of exegesis, interpretation, and application*. It is recurringly, "You have heard that it was said . . . but I say" (Matt 5:21-22). The key issue has to do with a flat, one-dimensional perspective that imagines the law to be a set of fixed rules to be applied to cases, a notion reflected in the foolish statement of one of the justices of the Supreme Court who proposed that a judge is "an umpire who calls balls and strikes." Such a comment fails to acknowledge the inescapable work of interpretation and the ways in which ideology covertly (well, sometimes covertly!) impinges upon law in the processes of interpretation. All such notions that the law has one "original meaning" are deeply misleading, as in the current fad of "originalism" in the practice of the court. That notion obviously translates into the preferences of the justice conveniently and predictably morphing into "original meaning," so that "preferences" are readily transposed into "givens" placed beyond question. So it is with those who want to take biblical law in a one-dimensional way as though it were a script for Medes and Persians, while completely neglecting the reality that the law is a concrete performance of a relationship of trust, loyalty, and fidelity.

There is, in current legal theory, a deep challenge to such a reductionist notion of law, as there must be a challenge in biblical interpretation. It is important that biblical exegetes and church interpreters should pay attention to this larger challenge concerning law, as we have a great stake in the conduct of that challenge. Thus, there is a powerful insistence in current legal theory that law is essentially an ongoing interpretive conversation that requires courage, freedom, imagination, and candor, one that refuses simplistic "application" of the "one meaning" of the law.

I am especially instructed by the work of James Boyd White, who has shown the way in which law participates in the imaginative rhetoric of poetry and narrative.[22] White writes:

The law is not an abstract system or scheme of rules, as we often speak of it, but an inherently unstable structure of thought and expression. It is built upon a distinct set of dynamic and dialogic tensions. . . . Legal thought is not the top-down elaboration of the meaning of a set of rules, by a process of logic or end-means rationality; nor is it a pattern of conduct that can be adequately represented and understood in the language of social science. . . . [It is] a way of managing the relations between what looks like a system and many dimensions of actual life. . . . I have been resisting an image of law as rules and policy, but behind those things is a deeper vision: of law as abstract, mechanical, impersonal, essentially bureaucratic in nature, narrowing rather than broadening the human capacity for experience, understanding, imagination, and empathy.[23]

White's preferred markers for law are "dynamic, dialogic, and unsettled." Such a characterization of law contradicts the Medes and the Persians of ancient time and their counterparts in our time. Those markers of law, moreover, are exactly what we have in the tradition of Deuteronomy that takes up the charter of Sinai and parses it in a dynamic way, in dialogue with new cultural challenges, and that keeps "turning to the right and to the left" in unsettled and unsettling ways. It is moreover a continuing practice of the rabbis, including Jesus, who took from his treasure "what is old and what is new" (Matt 13:51-53).

In his formidable study of Antigone, Julen Etxabe writes of this thick notion of law:

We must imagine a law that is enlivened by the myths and narratives that make it meaningful and the language that lends norms their full expressive force, enabling individuals to argue, modify, change, appeal, or defend those norms, and to persuade others about their interpretation, validity and pre-eminence. We are to conceive of a law constructed rhetorically, by way of conversations and exchanges, often of a polemic nature with others . . . as a kind of language (open-ended, flexible, and constantly evolving). This language is much richer than the image of law as the syllogistic application of rules would have us think, for it provides the entire arsenal for a full and flourishing normative life.[24]

He goes on to say,

> The structure of the *nomos* [a normative world] is not to be imagined as a pyramid in which each norm is validated by its immediate superior until we reach the highest normative step of the ladder. The picture is rather one of an enmeshed web of narratives around a possible, plausible, and desirable state of affairs, which are stored and brought to life by the usual processes of memory and recollection.[25]

The Torah of Israel is exactly such a web of narratives, voiced often as oracle, song, and litany. Reminiscent of the *shema'* of Deuteronomy is the accent on listening in this understanding of the law. Susan Bickford (quoted by Richard Dawson) says of such listening:

> Listening . . . involves an active willingness to construct certain relationships of attention . . . without moving ourselves toward the background, we cannot hear at all. . . . Political listening cannot be grounded in passivity or an absence of self, for politics itself requires precisely the opposite. . . . It is the *interaction* of our efforts that results in a decision, a joint action. . . . There must of course be an equality in terms of the role one plays. All must engage in shifting back and forth between perspectives, speaking and listening in turn.[26]

The convergence of conversation and listening means, inescapably, that law requires immense and daring imagination. Martha Nussbaum has shown in detailed ways how it is that imagination is operative in good law.[27] Of course Darius had no notion of listening, conversation, or imagination. But of course he did not prevail, for his *nomos* (authorized world) was defeated by the *nomos* of Yhwh that remained more authoritatively resilient than the codes of empire. The *nomos* of Yhwh operates in the orbit of grace and justice. It is unfortunate, both in our Reformation traditions and in the anxious, reductionist "constitutionalism" in our society, that law has been so badly caricatured. Law in Israel is indeed conversation between the God of grace and justice and those who find great joy in being party to that conversation of speaking and hearing. It is a conversation that evokes fresh glad obedience that had not yet occurred to Moses, or even to Jesus; it is the continuing work of the Spirit. The practical question concerns who is permitted to participate in that continuing interpretive conversation.[28] What can be better than to hear and answer back in fidelity! In such a way, says White,

> there is always the possibility that one can bring the world into new life.[29]

NOTES

INTRODUCTION

1 On Solomon's regime and its theological significance in Israel, see Walter Brueggemann, *Solomon: Israel's Ironic Icon of Human Achievement* (Columbia: University of South Carolina Press, 2005).

2 See James Boyd White, *Living Speech: Resisting the Empire of Force* (Princeton: Princeton University Press, 2006).

3 Roland Boer, *The Sacred Economy of Ancient Israel* (Louisville, Ky.: Westminster John Knox, 2015), 210.

4 Note two matters in this statement. First, in what follows I do not speak of the entire Old Testament that itself offers many problems for our exposition. I speak only of a particular trajectory of texts and interpretation. Second, in using the phrase "good news," I fully acknowledge that the "good news" as understood in the Christian "gospel" and the good news that Judaism finds in the text are very different and should not be conflated. Both nonetheless arise from the fidelity of God.

5 The implication of Yhwh in violence is an immense problem of interpretation concerning which we have an important and growing interpretive corpus. Among the best of this growing

corpus is Jerome F. D. Creach, *Violence in Scripture* (Louisville, Ky.: Westminster John Knox, 2013).

6 For a critical analysis of the downside of globalization, see Enrique Dussel, *Ethics of Liberation in the Age of Globalization and Exclusion* (Durham, N.C.: Duke University Press, 2013).

7 Fox Butterfield, *All God's Children: The Bosket Family and the American Tradition of Violence* (New York: Knopf, 1995).

1: THE NATURE AND MISSION OF GOD

1 David J. A. Clines, "Hosea 2: Structure and Interpretation," in *Studia Biblica 1978*, JSOTSup 11 (Sheffield: JSOT Press, 1979).

2 Phyllis Trible, *God and the Rhetoric of Sexuality*, OBT (Philadelphia: Fortress, 1978), ch. 2.

3 See Nathan C. Lane, *The Compassionate but Punishing God: A Canonical Analysis of Exodus 34:6-7* (Eugene, Ore.: Pickwick, 2010).

4 See Walter Brueggemann, "On 'Being Human' in the Psalms," in *Oxford Handbook of the Psalms* (Oxford: Oxford University Press, 2014), 515–28.

5 See Jer 24:7; 30:22; 31:33; Ezek 11:20; 24:11; 36:28; 37:18, 23, 27.

6 William P. Brown, *Wisdom's Wonder: Character, Creation, and Crisis in the Bible's Wisdom Literature* (Grand Rapids: Eerdmans, 2014), 6–7, reports that Joseph Ewen classifies characters along three axes: complexity, development, and penetration into the "inner life." One can see all of these markings in the portrayal of Yhwh in the text.

7 Douglas F. Ottati, *Theology for Liberal Protestants: God the Creator* (Grand Rapids: Eerdmans, 2013), 54 passim.

8 Jack Miles, *God: A Biography* (New York: Knopf, 1995), has traced the way in which the character and agency of God disappears in the later traditions of the Old Testament.

9 Claus Westermann, *Praise and Lament in the Psalms* (Atlanta: John Knox, 1981); see also Patrick D. Miller, *They Cried to the Lord: The Form and Theology of Biblical Prayer* (Minneapolis: Augsburg Fortress, 1994), chaps. 2–3.

10 See John Barton, *Understanding Old Testament Ethics* (Louisville, Ky.: Westminster John Knox, 2003), 50–54.

11 More than anyone else, Emmanuel Levinas, *Totality and Infinity: An Essay on Exteriority* (Pittsburgh: Duquesne University Press, 1969), has shown how the "other" is decisive for human life.

12 Patrick D. Miller, *Israelite Religion and Biblical Theology: Collected Essays*, JSOTSup 267 (Sheffield: Sheffield Academic, 2000), 599.

13 Martha C. Nussbaum, *The Clash Within: Democracy, Religious Violence, and India's Future* (Cambridge, Mass.: Harvard University Press, 2007), 337.

14 Hans Heinrich Schmid, *Gerechtigkeit als Weltordnung: Hintergrund und Geschichte des alttestamentlichen Gerechtigkeitsbegriffes* (Tubingen: Mohr, 1968); *Wesen und Geschichte der Weisheit: Eine Untersuchung zur altorientalischen und israelitischen Weisheitsliteratur*, BZAW 101 (Berlin: Töpelmann, 1966).

15 Hans Heinrich Schmid, "Creation, Righteousness, and Salvation: 'Creation Theology' as the Broad Horizon of Biblical Theology," in *Creation in the Old Testament*, IRT 6, ed. Bernhard W. Anderson (Philadelphia: Fortress, 1984), 102–17; Rolf P. Knierim, *The Task of Old Testament Theology: Substance, Method, and Cases* (Grand Rapids: Eerdmans, 1995).

2: JUSTICE

1 Jacques Derrida, "'Force of Law': The Mystical Foundation of Authority," *Cardozo Law Review* 11 (1990): 919–1045. The journal has not been available to me, but I here depend on John Caputo, *Demythologizing Heidegger* (Bloomington: University of Indiana Press, 1993), 193.

2 Sigmund Mowinckel, *Psalmenstudien II: Das Thronbesteigungsfest Jahwas und der Ursprung der Eschatologie* (Christiania [Oslo]: Jacob Dybwad, 1922). His hypothesis has recently received important support from J. J. M. Roberts, "Mowinckel's Enthronement Festival: A Review," in *The Book of Psalms: Composition and Reception*, ed. Peter W. Flint and Patrick D. Miller Jr. (Leiden: Brill, 2005), 97–115.

3 Walter Brueggemann, *Israel's Praise: Doxology against Idolatry and Ideology* (Philadelphia: Fortress, 1988), chap. 1.

4 Hans Heinrich Schmid, *Gerechtigkeit als Weltordnung: Hintergrund und Geschichte des alttestamentlichen Gerechtigkeitsbegriffes* (Tubingen: Mohr, 1968).

5 Claus Westermann, "The Way of Promise through the Old Testament," in *The Old Testament and Christian Faith: A Theological Discussion*, ed. Bernhard W. Anderson (New York: Harper &

Row, 1963), 200–24; idem., *Blessing in the Bible and the Life of the Church*, OBT (Philadelphia: Fortress, 1978).

6 On the paradigmatic nature of the narrative, see Erich Voegelin, *Israel and Revelation* (Baton Rouge: Louisiana State University Press, 1956).

7 Leon R. Kass, *The Beginning of Wisdom: Reading Genesis* (New York: Free Press, 2003), 569 passim.

8 James C. Scott, *Weapons of the Weak: Everyday Forms of Resistance* (New Haven, Conn.: Yale University Press, 1985); idem, *Domination and the Arts of Resistance: Hidden Transcripts* (New Haven, Conn.: Yale University Press, 1990).

9 See Michael Hardt and Antonio Negri, *Multitude: War and Democracy in the Age of Empire* (New York: Penguin Books, 2004).

10 Terry Eagleton, *Reason, Faith, and Revolution: Reflections on the God Debate* (New Haven, Conn.: Yale University Press, 2009).

11 Eagleton, *Reason, Faith, and Revolution*, 10.

12 Eagleton, *Reason, Faith, and Revolution*, 14.

13 Eagleton, *Reason, Faith, and Revolution*, 20.

14 Eagleton, *Reason, Faith, and Revolution*, 23.

15 Enrique Dussel, *Ethics of Liberation: In the Age of Globalization and Exclusion* (Durham, N.C.: Duke University Press, 2013).

16 Dussel, *Ethics of Liberation*, 243.

17 Dussel, *Ethics of Liberation*, 242–43.

18 Dussel, *Ethics of Liberation*, 244.

19 Dussel, *Ethics of Liberation*, 244.

20 See the somewhat different angle on this question by Hartmut Gese, *Essays on Biblical Theology* (Minneapolis: Augsburg Fortress, 1981), 82–83:

> Accordingly we can distinguish in the Old Testament between Zion Torah and Sinai Torah. . . . We have reached the end of the Old Testament and in conclusion we may ask how the distinction between Sinai Torah and Zion Torah and the expectation of an eschatological Torah revelation affected Israel's existence in late Old Testament times.

21 On this text, see Georg Fohrer, "The Righteous Man in Job 31," in *Essays in Old Testament Ethics*, ed. James L. Crenshaw and John T. Willis (New York: KTAV, 1974), 1–22.

3: GRACE

1 Morton Smith, "The Common Theology of the Ancient Near East," *JBL* 71 (1952): 135–47.

2 Norman K. Gottwald, *The Tribes of Yahweh: A Sociology of Religion in Liberated Israel 1250–1050 B.C.E.* (Maryknoll, N.Y.: Orbis, 1979), 670–78.

3 Erhard S. Gerstenberger, *Theologies in the Old Testament*, trans. John Bowden (Minneapolis: Augsburg Fortress, 2002), 207–72.

4 Walter Brueggemann, *Old Testament Theology: Essays on Structure, Theme, and Text* (Minneapolis: Augsburg Fortress, 1992), 1–21.

5 See Claus Westermann, *Basic Forms of Prophetic Speech*, trans. Hugh Clayton White (Philadelphia: Westminster, 1967).

6 Gerhard von Rad, *Wisdom in Israel* (Nashville: Abingdon, 1972).

7 Klaus Koch, "Is There a Doctrine of Retribution in the Old Testament?" in *Theodicy in the Old Testament*, ed. James L. Crenshaw, IRT 4 (Philadelphia: Fortress, 1983), 57–87.

8 Patrick D. Miller Jr., *Sin and Judgment in the Prophets: A Stylistic and Theological Analysis*, SBLMS 27 (Chico, Calif.: Scholars Press, 1982).

9 Erhard Gerstenberger, *Wesen und Herkunft des sogenannten apodiktischen Rechts im Alten Testament* (Bonn: Rheinischen Friedrich-Wilhelms-Univesität, 1961), argues vigorously that the apodictic "Thou shalt not" is rooted in family and clan wisdom.

10 Hans Walter Wolff, "The Kerygma of the Deuteronomistic Historical Work," in *The Vitality of Old Testament Traditions*, ed. Walter Brueggemann and Hans Walter Wolff (Atlanta: John Knox, 1975), 83–100.

11 See Michael Fishbane, *Biblical Interpretation in Ancient Israel* (Oxford: Clarendon, 1985), 307–12.

12 See Paul Joyce, *Divine Initiative and Human Response in Ezekiel*, JSOTSup 51 (Sheffield: JSOT Press, 1989), 35–60.

13 See Walter Brueggemann, "The Travail of Pardon: Reflections on *slh*," in *A God So Near: Essays on Old Testament Theology in Honor of Patrick D. Miller*, ed. Brent A. Strawn and Nancy R. Bowen (Winona Lake, Ind.: Eisenbrauns, 2003), 283–97.

14 Jacqueline Lapsley (*Can These Bones Live? The Problem of the Moral Self in the Book of Ezekiel*, BZAW 301 [Berlin: de Gruyter, 2000]) has probed the way in which Ezekiel moves from a sturdy call to repentance to a free gift of restoration.

15 See Todd Gitlin and Liel Leibovitz, *Chosen Peoples: America, Israel, and the Ordeals of Divine Election* (New York: Simon & Schuster, 2010).

16 The familiar hymn has words by Stuart K. Hine; see *Glory to God* (Louisville, Ky.: Westminster John Knox, 2013), hymn 625.

17 See Gottwald, *Tribes of Yahweh*, 679–91.

18 Brueggemann, *Old Testament Theology*, 22–44.

19 See Rainer Albertz, "How Radical Must the New Beginning Be? The Discussion between the Deutero-Isaiah and the Ezekiel School," in *The Centre and the Periphery: A European Tribute to Walter Brueggemann*, ed. Jill Middlemas, David J. A. Clines, and Else K. Holt (Sheffield: Sheffield Phoenix, 2010), 7–21.

20 The phrase "commutative justice" is from Hayek. See Ched Myers and Matthew Colwell, *Our God Is Undocumented: Biblical Faith and Immigrant Justice* (Maryknoll, N.Y.: Orbis, 2012), 174:

> Under capitalism, justice is reduced to its commutative form. That is, justice is a matter of rendering what is due in accord with the provisions of contracts freely entered into. There is, as Hayek insists, no such thing as social justice, by which he means any kind of moral norm that should guide the distribution of resources in a society beyond the commutative justice of market exchanges. Or, as another economist has it more directly, "an unfettered market system shows no mercy."

And this from Daniel M. Bell Jr., *The of Desire: Christianity and Capitalism in a Postmodern World* (Grand Rapids: Baker Academic, 2012), 109:

> Under capitalism, justice is strictly personal or "commutative." That is to say, justice is solely a matter of enforcing the terms of voluntary, contractual exchange. Justice does not mandate that those exchanges result in a particular outcome or even that exchanges be made in the first place, All justice entails is the maintenance of the space for the possibility of voluntary (i.e., noncoercive) exchanges, which it does by enforcing the rules of contracts and property.

21 Claus Westermann, *Genesis 1–11: A Commentary* (Minneapolis: Augsburg, 1984), 166–67.

22 This is a reference that is lost to me. But see the way in which Phyllis Trible (*God and the Rhetoric of Sexuality*, OBT [Philadelphia: Fortress, 1978]) shrewdly juxtaposes Genesis 2–3 ("A Love Story Gone Awry," 72–143) with the Song of Solomon ("Love's Lyrics Redeemed," 144–65).

23 The two characteristics that characterize the righteous, "gracious, merciful" (*hannan, raham*), are expressed in quite strong terms.

4: LAW

1 See Robert Williamson Jr., "God in Crisis: A Re-reading of Genesis 22" (forthcoming).

2 See Nathan C. Lane, *The Compassionate, but Punishing God: A Canonical Analysis of Exodus 34:6-7* (Eugene, Ore.: Pickwick, 2010).

3 See Michelle Alexander, *The New Jim Crow: Mass Incarceration in the Age of Colorblindness* (New York: New Press, 2010); and Joseph Margulies, *What Changed When Everything Changed: 9/11 and the Making of National Identity* (New Haven, Conn.: Yale University Press, 2013).

4 See Robert M. Cover, "The Supreme Court, 1982 Term—Foreword: Nomos and Narrative," *Harvard Law Review* 97 (1983): 4–68.

5 See Terry Eagleton, *Reason, Faith, and Revolution: Reflections on the God Debate* (New Haven, Conn.: Yale University Press, 2009).

6 Acknowledgment should of course be made of Noachian laws that pertain to Gentiles. See David Novak, *The Image of the Non-Jew in Judaism: An Historical and Constructive Study of the Noahide Laws*, Toronto Studies in Theology 14 (Toronto: Edwin Mellen, 1983).

7 See Walter Brueggemann, "The Countercommands of Sinai," in *Disruptive Grace: Reflections on God, Scripture, and the Church*, ed. Carolyn J. Sharp (Minneapolis: Augsburg Fortress, 2011), 75–92. For my more general statement on obedience and law, see Brueggemann, *Old Testament Theology: An Introduction*, Library of Biblical Theology (Nashville: Abingdon, 2008).

8 Martin Noth, *The Laws in the Pentateuch and Other Studies* (Philadelphia: Fortress, 1967), 51.

9 Emmanuel Levinas, *Totality and Infinity: An Essay on Exteriority*, trans. Alphonso Lingis (Pittsburgh: Duquesne University Press, 1969).

10 William T. Cavanaugh, *Torture and Eucharist: Theology, Politics, and the Body of Christ*, Challenges in Contemporary Theology (Oxford: Blackwell, 1998).

11 Patrick D. Miller Jr., "The Human Sabbath: A Study in Deuteronomic Theology," *Princeton Theological Seminary Bulletin* 6 (1985): 81–97.

12 See Walter Brueggemann, *Interpretation and Obedience: From Faithful Reading to Faithful Living* (Minneapolis: Augsburg Fortress, 1991), 145–58.

13 On the critical issues at stake, see Douglas A. Knight, *Law, Power, and Justice in Ancient Israel*, Library of Ancient Israel (Louisville, Ky.: Westminster John Knox, 2011).

14 See Jeffries M. Hamilton, *Social Justice and Deuteronomy: The Case of Deuteronomy 15*, SBLDS 136 (Atlanta: Scholars Press, 1992).

15 S. A. Kaufman, "The Structure of the Deuteronomic Law," *Maarav* 1 (1978–1979): 105–58; Georg Braulik, "The Sequence of the Laws in Deuteronomy 12–26 and in the Decalogue," in *A Song of Power and the Power of Song: Essays on the Book of Deuteronomy*, ed. Duane L. Christensen (Winona Lake, Ind.: Eisenbrauns, 1993), 313–35; John H. Walton, "The Decalogue Structure of the Deuteronomic Law," in *Interpreting Deuteronomy: Issues and Approaches*, ed. David G. Firth and Philip S. Johnson (Downers Grove, Ill.: IVP Academic, 2012), 93–117.

16 Frank Crüsemann, *The Torah: Theology and Social History of Old Testament Law* (Edinburgh: T&T Clark, 1996), 224.

17 Patrick D. Miller, "Deuteronomy and Psalms: Evoking a Biblical Conversation," in *Israelite Religion and Biblical Theology: Collected Essays*, JSOTSup 267 (Sheffield: Sheffield Academic, 2000), 318–36.

18 D. W. Winnicott, *The Maturational Processes and the Facilitating Environment: Studies in the Theory of Emotional Development* (Madison, Conn.: International Universities Press, 1965), 140–52 passim.

19 Philip P. Hallie, *Lest Innocent Blood Be Shed: The Story of the Village of Le Chambon and How Goodness Happened There* (New York: Harper, 1994).

20 Elie Wiesel, *The Jews of Silence: A Personal Report on Soviet Jewry* (London: Vallentine Mitchell, 1968), 46–49.

21 Wiesel, *Jews of Silence*, 49.

22 James Boyd White, *The Legal Imagination*, abr. ed. (Chicago: Chicago University Press, 1985), 207–95. I am much indebted to Professor White for this part of my discussion.

23 James Boyd White, "An Old-Fashioned View of the Nature of Law," *Theoretical Inquiries in Law* 12 (2011): 381, 397, 400, 402.

24 Julen Etxabe, *The Experience of Tragic Judgment* (New York: Routledge, 2013), 7, 23.

25 Etxabe, *Tragic Judgment*, 25.

26 Susan Bickford, *The Dissonance of Democracy: Listening, Conflict, and Citizenship* (Ithaca, N.Y.: Cornell University Press, 1996), 12, 146–47; quoted by Richard Dawson, *Justice as Attunement: Transforming Constitutions in Law, Literature, Economics and the Rest of Life* (New York: Routledge, 2014), 10–11.

27 Martha Nussbaum, *Poetic Justice: The Literary Imagination and Public Life* (Boston: Beacon, 1995). She offers a riff on Walt Whitman's "Poet as Judge" on pp. 82, 99:

> In particular, I shall contrast the literary judge with three rivals: a judge who cultivates skeptical detachment, a judge who conceives of judicial reasoning on the model of formal reasoning in the sciences, and a judge who cultivates a lofty distance from particulars for reasons of judicial neutrality. I shall argue that the literary judge has good reasons for eschewing skeptical detachment and for preferring to quasi-scientific models an evaluative humanistic form of practical reasoning; these reasons are deeply rooted in the common-law tradition. She does not pursue neutrality, but in a manner that coheres with our account of the judicious spectator in chapter 3, requiring, rather than forbidding, sympathetic knowledge of value-laden human facts. . . . The ability to think of people's lives in the novelist's way is, Breyer argues, an important part of the equipment of a judge. A part and not, obviously, the whole, not even the central part—but a vital part nonetheless. This claim is the more impressive in that it comes from a judge who is far from being a sentimentalist, whose technical proficiency is great, and who is, if anything, considered more intellectual

than emotional. Even a judge so unsentimental, with such deep technical and intellectual commitments, then, grants that novel-reading is relevant to the judicial imagination.

28 One striking example of the way in which a new entrant into the interpretive conversation evokes new interpretations of Torah is the narrative account of the daughters of Zelophehad who are remembered by name in Numbers 27:2: Mahlah, Noah, Hoglah, Milcah, and Tirzah. The narrative is terse but clear:

> Then the daughters of Zelophehad came forward. . . . They said, ". . . Why should the name of our father be taken away from his clan because he had no son? Give to us a possession among our father's brothers." (vv. 1-2, 4)

In response to their insistence, Moses makes an interpretive reach:

> The daughters of Zelophehad are right in what they are saying; you shall indeed let them possess an inheritance among their father's brothers and pass the inheritance of their father on to them. (v. 7)

It seems clear that such a ruling was not available to Moses and would not have occurred to Moses until the daughters came forward with their claim. I am grateful to Davis Hankins for this remarkable example of new interpretation of Torah made possible and necessary by new participants in the interpretive conversation.

29 White, "Old-Fashioned View," 402.

SCRIPTURE INDEX

AUTHOR/SUBJECT INDEX